Disciples

Disciples

Reclaiming Our Identity, Reforming Our Practice

MICHAEL KINNAMON
JAN LINN

CHALICE
PRESS

ST. LOUIS, MISSOURI

Cover and interior design: Elizabeth Wright

Visit Chalice Press on the World Wide Web at
www.chalicepress.com

10 9 8 7 6 5 4 3 2 1   09 10 11 12 13 14

Library of Congress Cataloging–in–Publication Data

Kinnamon, Michael.
  Disciples : reclaiming our identity, reforming our practice / by
Michael Kinnamon and Jan G. Linn.
      p. cm.
  ISBN 978-0-8272-0635-9
  1. Disciples of Christ—Doctrines. I. Linn, Jan. II. Title.

BX7321.3.K56 2009
286.6'3—±dc   222009008693

Printed in the United States of America

Contents

Preface

Why a book like this, living as we do in a post-denominational age? You have asked a *legitimate* question. A Pew Forum on Religion and Public Life survey released in February of 2008 confirmed what church leaders have known for a long time, that the phenomenon of lay Christians "switching" churches without concern for denominational affiliation is commonplace. Baptists become Catholics, Catholics join up with Pentecostals, Protestants across the board switch from one church to another, and the percentage of people who have no religious affiliation has doubled in the last ten years.[1] At a time like this, why a book about the American-born denomination called the Christian Church (Disciples of Christ)?

Each chapter that follows provides a part of the overall answer to this question, but together all of them reflect the driving force behind this book. Both of us love this denomination we call home and believe it has a vital role to play in American religious life in the twenty-first century. At the same time, we see serious issues and problems in our life together that need churchwide attention and resolution. Our commitment to being Disciples compels us to offer a constructive critique of the beliefs and practices that make us who we are as a church. This is especially the case since we are convinced that denominations are not as irrelevant to the lives of all Christians as most believe, and are far from being extinct. Robert Wuthnow may well be correct in his assessment that clergy must now carry the primary responsibility for the future of denominations, but tradition remains important for all people of faith as they adapt to changing circumstances in an age in which the rapidity of change has become a permanent reality.[2] When understood, tradition provides stability as communities change. Change and tradition are not competitors, and certainly not antagonists.

They must coexist for the former to have direction and the latter to have meaning.

One thing that is obvious about the history of the Christian Church (Disciples of Christ) is that we have been an adaptable community. Neither the Disciples of Pennsylvania nor the Christians of Kentucky knew what the future held as they followed the imperative to overcome the scandal of denominationalism. That is not surprising, given the fact that our early leaders chose not to build on creedal faith as the means for uniting all Christians, or rely on known ecclesial structures and patterns of the past. Innovation was the direct by-product of their decision to forge a new path in America. Innovation requires a spirit of adaptability, a willingness to respond appropriately to the circumstances being confronted.

As will become evident in the chapters to follow, we believe a spirit of innovation lies at the heart of what we see for our community of faith as our own future unfolds. Without it we will be held back by old ways of thinking and acting that cannot confront the particular challenges the twenty-first century presents, the specifics of which will be discussed in detail in the pages that follow. The Lord of the church stays the same yesterday, today, and forever. Everything else is in flux. Our first leaders knew this, along with those who have pointed the way in each new generation of Disciples. It is more true today than ever, we think. But change has never been anything that has caused Disciples to cower or fear. Our trust is in God and not ourselves. We offer the best thinking and living we can as an offering to the One who can take our meager gifts and turn them into enough to meet the needs of many, even as he did on a hillside with a few loaves and fish a little boy gave to him years ago.

Journey is the metaphor that undergirds our effort to highlight the particularities of our identity and to make suggestions for revising and adapting the practices of our church. Our past is a proud one precisely because those in leadership then were willing to follow their vision of what it meant to be church in their own time in history. They would want us to do no less. In this spirit we invite the socially, politically, geographically, and theologically diverse people we are as the Christian Church (Disciples of Christ) into this discussion about the beliefs that reveal who we are and the practices that express our faithful living.

To this end, we decided early in the process that the chapters each of us would write needed to draw from our own understandings and experiences without seeking to harmonize any difference in perspectives there might be on the subjects we discuss. The thumbprint of each of us will be discernable throughout the book to anyone who is familiar with our previous writings, both in what is said and what is omitted in the various chapters, yet not in a way that prevents us from speaking with one voice on the major themes we present. One of the reasons we decided to write this book together is that through the many years in which we have been both colleagues and friends we have experienced the empowering truth that differences need not be cause for division. This book is a way we could say that we believe this is also true for the community of people called Disciples.

CHAPTER 1

Why We Are Disciples

Universals are always known in *particular* ways. We understand what discrimination means through particular experiences of it. We know what love is because of the particular people we have loved and who have loved us.

So it is with God. *God* is the word English-speaking believers use for the universal Creator and Sustainer of all that is. We who are Christians have come to know this God of all through God's particular incarnation in Jesus of Nazareth, the One we call Savior and Lord. The gospel according to John, in its opening lines, sets forth this central Christian conviction: "In the beginning was the Word, and the Word was with God, and the Word was God... And the Word became flesh and lived among us, and we have seen his glory, the glory as of a father's only son, full of grace and truth" (1:1, 14). In him, we experience God as compassionate and reconciling, as one who eats with outcasts, forgives the prodigal, and loves us even to the point of death on a cross.

In the same way, Jesus Christ is known to Christians down the street and around the world through particular traditions, traditions that are shaped by distinctive histories, cultures, and shared experiences. The authors of this book, a pastor and a professor, give thanks that we have come to have faith in Jesus Christ (and, thus, in God) within the tradition known as the Christian Church (Disciples of Christ)—often known simply as Disciples. This is certainly not the only way to be Christian! We have found, however that this particular heritage has great strengths that can give powerful witness to Christ in the twenty-first century, as it has for the past two hundred years. This book is, in effect, our testimony to why we are Disciples.

The Paradox of Disciples Identity

That said, it is important at the beginning to take note of the paradox that runs throughout Disciples history. On the one hand, we are a *church*; we gather for worship, engage in mission, baptize, ordain, and develop structures needed for common life. On the other hand, our Disciples forebears did not set out to be another American denomination—brand Z on a shelf that already has A through Y. We have seen ourselves as a reforming *movement* within the universal church, a movement whose reason for being is to help heal the church's divisions for the sake of its witness to the gospel of reconciliation. In the words of a recent document from the Disciples Vision Team, "We are Disciples of Christ, a movement for wholeness in a fragmented world."[1]

This is one major reason the authors of this book love being part of this church/movement. At our best, Disciples have been a very rare thing: a community with a deep sense of particular identity that isn't sectarian—because its particular identity is to be a healer of the universal church! Disciples have developed distinctive practices and perspectives (several of which we will explore in this book), not to separate ourselves from other Christians, but to offer these practices and perspectives as gifts for the renewal of Christ's one body.

This paradox, however, has often made it difficult for Disciples to say who we are. Our key early leaders, Alexander Campbell and Barton Stone, favored generic names—"Disciples" and "Christians"—to emphasize our place within the entire family of Christ's followers. The Disciples convention of 1909 (to which we will return below) declared that our movement "stands for the rejection of all party names in religion," so that even our label might show the preeminence of Christ. The irony, of course, is that our very commitment to the unity of the church is itself a distinguishing mark, a particular identity! Beyond that, how will people hear our witness to unity if we aren't clear about who we are and what we stand for?

Reclaiming Disciples Identity

The purpose of this book is to reclaim the identity of the Disciples movement in a way that encourages reform of our worship, fellowship, and mission. This seems like an ideal time for such an effort, in that 2009 marks the bicentennial of the seminal document of our tradition, the *Declaration and Address,* written by Thomas Campbell. This text, more than any other, has set the direction for our corporate identity. We make reference to it at various places in this volume.

In 1909, participants in the Disciples International Convention celebrated the centennial of Campbell's work by specifying, for their own era, "the chief things for which this movement stands." One of them—"the complete dominance of Christianity in our social, domestic, industrial, and political life, so that ours shall be indeed a Christian civilization"—will sound far too triumphalistic for many contemporary Disciples, given our positive experience of religious diversity. We suspect, however, that the rest of their list will ring true for Disciples today:

- We stand for the unity of the church and for "the manifestation of the spirit of unity by cooperation with other followers of Christ, who stand not with us in all things, but who hold to Christ as their head."
- We stand for the rejection of creeds as the basis of Christian unity and fellowship. More positively, we affirm (a) the Good Confession made by Peter—"You are the Messiah,

the Son of the Living God" (Mt. 16:16)—as the rock on which Jesus will build his church, and (b) the Bible as the only authoritative rule of faith and practice. Christian faith is trust in the person of Jesus Christ (as witnessed to in scripture), not in doctrines about him—which are often divisive.

- We stand for "Christian liberty," for freedom from ecclesiastical coercion "that has sought to make [people] think alike and worship alike, mistaking uniformity for unity."
- We stand for the organization of the church into congregations that have the right of self-governance "in all matters that pertain to their local welfare," but also for "the fellowship of all these churches together in the common work of advancing the kingdom of God." It is not in isolated efforts but through collaboration as members of a common body that congregations can "accomplish the work which Christ has laid upon his church, and promote their own spiritual development."
- We stand for the centrality of baptism and the Lord's Supper in the life of the church and for the restoration of their scriptural meaning and practice—including baptism that involves "the burial in water of a penitent believer" who signifies a willingness to walk in obedience to Christ, weekly celebration of the holy meal, and a table open to "all who believe in and love our Lord Jesus Christ."
- We stand for evangelization through the simple preaching of the gospel, avoiding methods that "dishonor God's character."[2]

Several things strike us about this naming of Disciples identity one hundred years ago. First, it demonstrates the stability of our heritage. Disciples, for all of our commitment to freedom and diversity, have developed a distinctive and enduring set of communal practices and theological perspectives. At the 2007 Disciples General Assembly, the Vision Team, created by the General Minister and President of the church, suggested twelve principles of identity that are remarkably consistent with those of the 1909 convention. They are:

1. We confess that Jesus is the Christ, the Son of the Living God, and proclaim him Lord and Savior of the world, requiring nothing more—and nothing less—as a basis of our life together.

2. We hold the centrality of scripture, recognizing that each person has the freedom—and the responsibility—to study God's Word within the community of the church.

3. We practice the baptism of believers, which emphasizes that God's grace demands a response of faith and discipleship, while also recognizing the baptism performed in other churches.

4. We gather for the Lord's Supper, as often as possible, experiencing at this table the gracious, forgiving presence of Jesus Christ.

5. We structure our community around the biblical idea of covenant, emphasizing not obedience to human authority but accountability to one another because of our shared obedience to Christ.

6. We participate in God's mission for the world, working with partners to heal the brokenness of creation and bring justice and peace to the whole human family.

7. We hear a special calling to make visible the unity of all Christians, proclaiming that in our diversity we belong to one another because we commonly belong to Christ.

8. We witness to the Gospel of God's saving love for the world in Jesus Christ, while continuing to struggle with how God's love may be known to others in different ways.

9. We affirm the priesthood of all believers, rejoicing in the gifts of the Holy Spirit—which include the gift of leadership—that God has given for the common good.

10. We celebrate the diversity of our common life, affirming our different histories, styles of worship, and forms of service.

11. We give thanks that each congregation, where Christ is present through faith, is truly the church, affirming as well that God's church and God's mission stretch from our doorsteps to the ends of the earth.
12. We anticipate God's coming reign, seeking to serve the God—Creator, Redeemer, and Sustainer—whose loving dominion has no end.[3]

This list puts more emphasis on lay ministry as a Disciple's distinctive (elders were generally ordained in nineteenth-century congregations) and gives more prominence to social justice as a dimension of Christian mission (the Social Gospel movement, which stressed that God's saving work is for societies as well as individuals, had not yet taken root). It is clear, however, that thoughtful Disciples in both eras stand for the same basic principles.

Disciples' Dynamic Identity

At the same time, ours is obviously a dynamic heritage that can adapt to new experiences. To take one example, the emphasis in 1909 on the cooperation of congregations in the mission of the church represents an important development beyond nineteenth-century congregationalism. With our Restructure in the 1960s, Disciples went further, disavowing the language of congregational "autonomy" and affirming that structures of common mission—regions, general units, the General Assembly—are, themselves, expressions of "church."

What we most appreciate, however, about the work of the 1909 convention is their insistence that Disciples identity is, most essentially, a matter of holding together what others frequently take to be either/or. The following sentence is illustrative. "The distinction between faith, which has Christ as its object, and opinions, which are deductions of human reason…has enabled the advocates of this Reformation to harmonize two important principles which have often been regarded as incompatible: namely, union and liberty."[4] It is not the commitment to freedom alone, or unity alone, that defines us; it is the combination that makes us who we are.

In the same way, Disciples are obviously not the only church to practice believers' baptism; but we are practically the only believers' baptism church to make Christian unity a key part of our mission and self-understanding. The commitments to radical discipleship (the point of this form of baptism) and ecumenical openness are generally seen as "either/or"; Disciples say "both/and." To take one other example, Disciples are obviously not the only church to make weekly celebration of the Lord's Supper central to its life and worship. We are practically the only one, however, to do so without a formal prayer book and ministerial hierarchy.

Throughout this book, we present evidence of this holding-in-tension identity and explore its implications for our practice as a community of faith. Perhaps the crucial tension, just below the surface in every chapter, is what we might call "bold humility": Disciples, at our best, have been both bold in our proclamation that Jesus Christ is Lord *and* humble in our willingness to receive gifts God has entrusted to other Christians and persons of other faiths. It is a major reason we are Disciples.

Need for Reform

But now the bad news. It should be clear to every observer that this reform movement called the Christian Church (Disciples of Christ) is, itself, in great need of reformation. We have not taught our own heritage to a new generation, to the point that even leaders in our congregations are unfamiliar with central aspects of our historical identity. Being a "restructured" denomination seems to have become an end in itself, with only a handful of practices to distinguish us from other churches. Having lay elders at the table, or baptizing pre-adolescents instead of babies, has become more of an idiosyncrasy—"just the way we do it"—than part of a theologically grounded effort to help renew the church universal. Even more troubling, many contemporary Disciples seem unaware of, or indifferent to, our special calling to promote Christian unity. Without this sense of calling, it is no wonder we are searching for direction and purpose—brand Z, without the historical depth of Presbyterians or the missional focus of Mennonites or the ethnic identity of Lutherans or the liturgical cohesion of Episcopalians.

In the chapters that follow, we offer an expanded diagnosis of these and other problems; but our real intent is constructive, not just diagnostic. This book is not a work of history or sociology, although it takes both seriously. We are arguing a case about how to reclaim the best of our heritage—our identity—to reform our practice for the sake of our mission. In short, we hope—as faithful, concerned members of this church—to name our problems clearly, reclaim our tradition intelligently, and look to God's future boldly.

We want to acknowledge one final paradox. Because of the problems faced by Disciples in these early years of the twenty-first century, this book concentrates on who we are as a movement; however, excessive focus on ourselves is, of course, the surest way not to focus on God—which, in the last analysis, is the heart of our problem! The great German theologian, Dietrich Bonhoeffer, saw this very clearly. "Our church," wrote Bonhoeffer from his cell in a Nazi prison, "has been fighting in these years only for its self-preservation, as though that were an end in itself, [and as a result] is incapable of taking the word of reconciliation and redemption to [humanity] and the world."[5] We believe that strengthening our own identity as disciples of Christ can enhance our participation in God's mission of peacemaking and compassionate service. Surely Bonhoeffer is right: a preoccupation with self-preservation is antithetical to a faith that has the cross as its central symbol. In Bonhoeffer's words, "the church is the church only when it exists for others,"[6]only when it gives itself away in witness, service, and advocacy. May it be so for us, for this movement called Disciples.

CHAPTER 2

Covenant

Freedom with Accountability

Freedom and community are two sides of the same coin. "The Stone-Campbell Movement," writes historian Leonard Allen, "whatever else one may say about it, began as a freedom movement, fully caught up in the heady excitement of 'freedom's ferment' in the early decades of American nationhood."[1] For far too long, said our founders, the church has been marked by patterns of teaching and decision-making that restrict legitimate diversity and stifle "the inalienable right of all laymen [and laywomen] to examine the sacred writings for themselves."[2] You can hear Thomas Campbell's passionate urgency, as well as his biblical grounding, in these lines from the 1809 *Declaration and Address*:

> Resume that precious, that dear bought, liberty wherewith Christ has made his people free; a liberty from subjection to any authority but his own, in matters of religion. Call no man father, no man master on earth; for one is your master, even Christ, and all ye are

brethren. Stand fast, therefore, in this precious liberty, and be not entangled again in the yoke of bondage.[3]

When, one hundred years later, Disciples celebrated the *Declaration and Address* as our movement's "declaration of independence," the centennial assembly (1909) reiterated that we stand for Christian liberty and against "a religious despotism that has sought to make men [and women] think alike and worship alike, mistaking uniformity for unity."[4] By then our protest had assumed a familiar form: no to ecclesiastical hierarchy that would impose decisions on congregations, no to creedal conformity that would regard particular statements of belief as tests of fellowship, and no to an elevation of clergy that would constrict the priesthood of all believers.

This well-known emphasis on freedom, however, is only half the picture. Disciples theologian Ralph Wilburn puts it this way: "From the beginning, Disciples of Christ have been aware of the need to hold this principle of individual freedom in creative balance with the principle of community."[5] Just as the apostle Paul admonished the new Christians in Galatia to exercise their freedom in Christ by becoming servants to one another (Gal. 5:1, 13), so the Disciples founders envisioned a freedom that would give rise to a "disciplined holiness"[6] sufficient to build up the one body of Christ. They clearly recognized that individual liberty, if unchecked by common submission to what the *Declaration and Address* calls the "self-evident" truths of scripture, undercuts the community's ability to live and witness together—thus threatening two other "pillars" of the movement: the unity of all Christians and their *mission* of calling the world to Jesus Christ.

Disciples in Tension between Freedom and Community

The questions this raises are obvious: Are the central themes of the Bible really so self-evident? What happens when Christians disagree about these truths? Isn't some form of teaching authority, some structure for decision-making, necessary to ensure the community's identity as a people of the gospel?

A demonstration of the complexity of this tension between freedom and community came early in the movement over the issue of slavery. Disciples abolitionists argued that slavery is a sin, inconsistent with the liberating gospel of our Savior, and should be taught as such by the church. Others, including Alexander Campbell, contended that scripture does not reject slavery per se and, thus, that Disciples could appropriately hold diverse opinions on the subject. While Campbell personally regarded slavery as "inexpedient," he cautioned, in the words of historian Paul Blowers, "against raising the civil liberties of slaves above the liberty (of social, political, and theological convictions) practiced and protected in the church."[7] Today we might well ask: Can community be authentic if its unity is preserved at the price of prophetic witness? Shouldn't the church have ways of speaking with authority on so momentous a matter? Doesn't the church community have a proper role in guiding the individual conscience?

Disciples leaders in the 1960s realized that these questions were pointing to a larger need within our denomination: to restructure ourselves in a way that preserved freedom without sacrificing community. Throughout the last half of the nineteenth century and the first half of the twentieth, Disciples had responded pragmatically (as we often do) to the tension between freedom and community, developing more or less formal structures for making decisions and doing mission together. Not until this substantial restructuring in the 1960s (often referred to as "Restructure") did Disciples attempt to address the issue theologically. The challenge was to find a middle ground, a foundation for being church, that promotes accountability without coercion, that calls church members to obedience to the gospel as articulated in community while still making plenty of room for dialogue, diversity, and dissent. The answer, according to the architects of Restructure, is the idea of covenant.

Disciples and Covenant

Covenant is a key term in scripture and also has figured prominently in the ecclesiology of various Reformation churches. We think its potential significance for Disciples can be clarified by naming four things that covenant is not.

First, a covenant is not simply an agreement among humans. *Covenant,* as used in scripture and the Reformed tradition, has both a vertical and a horizontal dimension because the God known to us in Jesus Christ is always a participant. That's why every serious church covenant emphasizes the authority of Christ, which strongly tempers freedom with responsibility. To put it another way, members of the covenant community are mutually accountable to one another because they are commonly accountable to Jesus Christ. The Reformed tradition doesn't speak of covenant as subordination to a superior authority or power but as ordination to communal discipleship by Christ who is the source of authority—not obedience to a human authority, but accountability to one another because of shared obedience to Christ.

Second, a covenant is not legalistic, not simply a list of things to do or not do. Rather, it involves a commitment "to walk together,"[8] seeking to conform ourselves as community— through prayer, study, and conversation—to the mind of Christ. It is a commitment to mutual accountability that presupposes a community intent on the study of scripture, intent on living a life centered on God, intent on recognizing God's grace in the other.

This means, of course, that a church built on covenant must accept, even value, diversity of perspective. The commitment we make is not always to agree, but to walk together as we attempt to discern where God would have us go. If the church is a purely voluntary association, then when we disagree we can simply take our marbles and leave. If, however, the church is a covenantal society constituted by God's initiative, then we stay at the table, especially when it is tough to do so. It almost goes without saying that this is not an easy way to be church(!), which may explain why so many Christians prefer more legalistic religion, and why Disciples have divided throughout our history.

Third, a covenant is not a contract. A contract emphasizes rights and involves "if/then" thinking: *If* you do this, *then* I will do that. By way of contrast, a covenant emphasizes responsibilities as well as rights and is based on "because/ therefore" thinking—which, of course, is the mindset of the gospel. Not "*if* I love my neighbor, *then* God will love me," but rather, "*because* God loves me, *therefore* I am freed from all the self-centered anxiety that keeps me from loving my neighbor." Because God has entered into covenant with us, marked by the blood of Christ, therefore we are freed to give our consent to a relationship of shared commitment—a relationship of grateful mutuality, not legal obligation.

Finally, a covenant has to do with freedom, but not freedom as our society generally understands it. In this culture, we tend to think of freedom as the ability to pursue one's own ends without external constraints; but that is not how the biblical writers or the Reformers saw it. Rather, freedom was the goal, the promise, of those who know the lordship of Christ. Covenant involves limitations, but they are limitations that lead to the real freedom of living no longer for ourselves. Because God alone is sovereign, the church is free of external control; but because Christ is Lord, the church willingly submits or conforms to him—which means treating others in community with great respect and seriousness as partners in the covenant.

Ronald Osborn, a central figure in the process of Restructure, once noted that the concept of covenant "occupied the Commission on Restructure more than any other theological idea."[9] Osborn also observed that at the last minute much of the explicit covenantal language was omitted from *The Design* of the Christian Church (Disciples of Christ)—in effect, the Church's constitution—because of a fear that courts would interpret it as contract, but we can still see the community's thinking in the wording of the Preamble to *The Design*: "The Christian Church

(Disciples of Christ) confesses Jesus Christ as Lord and constantly seeks in all its actions to be obedient to his authority... We commit ourselves to one another" (par. 2 and 3).[10]

Disciples' Restructure

Restructure, as we understand it, did not intend to drop liberty as an identity marker of our movement, but to revise it to mean "responsible freedom" (which is the essence of covenant). We Disciples had historically defined ourselves by what we were against: anti-creedal, anti-clerical, anti-ecclesiastical. Now was time for a positive conception of church, one that would allow us to hold one another accountable to shared mission and to decisions made in representative assemblies, without denying the legitimacy of dissent or the importance of theological diversity.

In this new church structure, every manifestation or expression of the church—congregational, regional, general—was given a particular responsibility to discern and respond to God's call, but to do so in covenantal interdependence. The General Assembly, for example, cannot dictate to the congregations, but neither are congregations free to ignore the corporate decision-making of the church in assembly. Majority decision-making is indicated in *The Design*; but, as Osborn put it, it is to be a majority of a particular kind of people—those who have pledged themselves to Christ and to one another and have sworn to conduct their lives according to the will of God set forth in scripture.

Behind all of this lies the assumption that the church doesn't only exist to meet our needs, to be a source of fellowship and occasional inspiration. Church is the place where we are shaped in a way of living that is likely not that of the world around us. The church should challenge our easy presuppositions and call us to intimate life with persons we, humanly speaking, may not like or be like. What the theology of covenant insists, however, is that this calling to account is not done by some "superior" authority but by ourselves through persons and bodies we authorize to help hold us accountable to our own covenantal promises.

That, at least, is the theory. As we look at the current situation, however, two things stand out. First, the cultural air that Disciples breathe in North America reinforces the tendency to exalt freedom at the expense of community. Robert Bellah and colleagues—in their seminal book, *Habits of the Heart*—conclude that most Americans no longer get moral instruction from character-forming community of any kind, including the church.[11] Many of us take our Christianity a la carte, picking and choosing those values and practices that justify our way of life, thinning out the gospel to fit our culturally shaped prejudices. Such extreme individualism obviously pulls the foundation out from under Christian education—which has declined markedly in mainline denominations.

These insights are supported by numerous scholars, including sociologists Dean Hoge, Benton Johnson, and Donald Luidens in their study of Presbyterian baby Boomers, entitled *Vanishing Boundaries*. The authors describe the prevalence of what they call "lay liberalism," the chief characteristic of which is an unwillingness to make authoritative claims in matters of faith or to accept the claims of others as authoritative. For lay liberals, they write, "preferences in religion are like preferences in art; since no agreed-upon authorities exist, questions of good or bad art and religion need to be decided by each individual on the basis of personal feelings."[12]

Baby Boomers tell the researchers that they are Christians because Christianity—or, at least, their version of it—is true for them; and they belong to a church because it meets their needs. Whenever these things are no longer the case, they simply stop going to church or move to another congregation.

To be sure, there is some backlash against all of this (although even conservative Protestant churches generally put few demands on their members); but the data on mainline denominations is overwhelming. Gary Dorrien summarizes the sociological literature this way:

These studies [from the 1980s and 1990s] repeatedly show that mainline churchgoers generally lack a deep or coherent faith, expect to be catered to, do not expect to be asked to do much [beyond giving money], feel little commitment to each other as participants in something greater than themselves, and consider social mission activities to be optional.[13]

Second, for whatever reasons—the legacy of freedom among Disciples, the individualism of the culture, the actual structure set up in the 1960s—Disciples, despite the rhetoric of Restructure, have not really taken covenant seriously as a basis of church life. On the more personal level, Disciples don't do a good job, in our experience, of teaching that baptism is an entry into covenantal relationship or that membership in a congregation involves covenantal responsibility or that biblical literacy is not optional, especially in a church that has jettisoned creeds, bishops, any form of magisterium, and formal liturgies. We often proclaim, in the words of one congregational brochure, that "Disciples believe in the freedom of every Christian to make his own decisions in matters of faith," instead of affirming that we believe in the great teachings of the biblical tradition—that God was in Christ reconciling the world to God's own self and making us ambassadors of reconciliation, that Christ is our peace who has broken down the dividing wall of hostility between former enemies—even as we protect, on biblical grounds, the right of each believer to interpret these statements of the gospel *in community*.

All of this has naturally impoverished our capacity to think theologically. Clark Williamson, longtime professor of theology at Christian Theological Seminary, states the issue powerfully:

We [Disciples] remembered the right of private inter-pretation more than the duty of it, and interpretation degenerated into mere opinion. Now we delight in a diversity of opinions, forgetting that to interpret is to understand, and that to understand is to be able to give reasons. Diverse understandings can be discussed in a community of faith. Opinions can merely be asserted. Consequently, moral stances as well as theological ones tend to be looked upon as opinions and as such make no claim on those who regard them.[14]

Anyone who has attended a Disciples General Assembly in recent years will recognize the truth of this characterization and appreciate how this tendency to hurl opinions rather than seek deeper common understanding through genuine dialogue undercuts our capacity to speak persuasively about the Good News.

On the more corporate level, Disciples have amended *The Design* to incorporate more covenantal language, including these new sentences: "We relate to each other in a covenantal manner, to the end that all expressions [of the church] will seek God's will and be faithful to God's mission. We are committed to mutual accountability." Such amendment, however, seems to have had little impact. From the perspective of the general units (and others), various regions have broken covenant by making unilateral decisions about the distribution of mission funds—decisions with obvious churchwide implications— unilaterally. From the perspective of the regions (and others), several general units have broken covenant by making unilateral decisions about program and finances, decisions with obvious churchwide implications, unilaterally. The attitude seems to be: When *you* do it, it is breaking covenant; when *we* do it, it is exercising appropriate freedom to oversee our own affairs! In any case, the tide of interdependence and mutual accountability, so touted at Restructure, is at low ebb.

Disciples Rethinking Restructure

In this environment, Disciples leaders discuss the need to rethink Restructure. Our perspective, however, is that the major problem with the idea of church set forth at Restructure is that we never really tried it!

"Covenant" provides Disciples with a framework for holding freedom and community in appropriate tension; but the theory and practice of covenant have not permeated the life of the church. We have been shaped far more by notions of American individualism than by biblical interdependence. And so the question is: How might we begin to change this situation? How might Disciples become a more covenantal people, a people more aware of our accountability to Christ and, therefore, to one another?

We are convinced that the reform or renewal of covenant will not happen—certainly not for Disciples!—in a top-down manner. Rather, if covenantal relations are strengthened, it will be through the renewal of particular practices—in congregations, in regions, in the general church. The following recommendations for such renewal are meant to be more suggestive than exhaustive. Readers may respond to some of them by saying, "There's no way that will ever fly!" or "We've been doing that for years!" But even such responses may be the start of a needed conversation.

Congregations have a number of obvious moments in which people enter into or reaffirm covenant with God and the community, including baptism, new membership, and the installation of a minister or congregational officers. How might we emphasize the mutually accountable character of these commitments? Many North American congregations have covenants that are given to new members. The covenantal language of a congregation to which one of the authors belongs can serve as an example:

> I covenant with _____ Christian Church and the Christian Church (Disciples of Christ) to become an active part of the worship, study, community life, and service of this congregation. I will strive to grow in my discipleship, offering my God-given time, talent, and resources to God's glory and the mission of the church.

While we wish it spoke first about God's covenant with us, this language has much to commend it—including a sense that each member enters into covenant with the whole church, not just this congregation.

Renewing the Covenant

The problem is that the covenant is read once, if that, and then set aside. What if it were publicly signed, regularly referred to, and liturgically renewed? What if the covenant were periodically read and members asked to reflect on how they have grown spiritually, on how they have contributed to building up the community, on how they have demonstrated love of neighbor? Disciples congregations don't have legal *requirements*, but shouldn't they have public *expectations* for life as followers of Christ? Shouldn't such expectations be taught in rigorous classes for all new members, not just in pastor's classes for youth about to be baptized?

In fact, this is the practice of the congregation to which the other author of this book belongs. This covenant, cited below, is reaffirmed on an annual basis during an annual "Covenant Renewal Service." In this way, the centrality of being a member of a covenant community is highlighted. Moreover, a usual practice is for one of the ministers to preach a series of sermons underlining the different dimensions of the covenant pledge weeks in advance of the renewal service.

By God's grace given in and through Jesus Christ, whom we have confessed as Savior and Lord of our life, we joyfully commit ourselves to being a member of the _____ T.E.A.M.

This means for this year we are willing to give our Time in attendance, our Energy in ministry, our Attention in prayer and study, and our Money in support, all to the building up of this community of faith and its witness to Jesus Christ in the world.

In making this covenant we are consciously pledging to love and serve the Lord, and to trust the Holy Spirit to lead us in all things to witness to our faith through word and deed.

If there should be times when we feel like we are being stretched in uncomfortable ways, we will also trust the Spirit to use them to nudge us toward deeper spiritual maturity.

May God bless all of us who share life and ministry together here at _____, that together we may be a blessing to others.

Another worship experience that can be used to emphasize the covenant nature of congregational life is the installation of a new pastor. In this regard, we appreciate the language of congregational response found in *Chalice Worship*: "We covenant to uphold our pastor with our prayers, to share *her/his* joys and sorrows, to attend to *her/his* preaching and teaching of God's word, to welcome *her/his* pastoral care, and to honor *her/his* leadership."[15] Congregations usually have ways to evaluate how the minister is living up to his or her commitments; but what if the elders periodically took stock of how the congregation is living up to its covenantal promises? Church members have a right to expect their minister to be a teacher of the Christian faith, one who regularly spends time in the study of scripture and in prayerful reflection on its meaning for our lives. But ministers also have a right to expect church members to take the ministers' teaching very seriously—even when (especially when!) they tackle controversial topics.

Unfortunately, the recommended baptismal service in *Chalice Worship* does not reflect such an entry into a covenant of mutual accountability. Again, however, the bigger problem has to do with the remembrance of it. What if persons were expected, on the one-year anniversary of their baptism, to testify publicly to what it has meant in their lives? What if ministers made it a point to find out when members were baptized and to celebrate tenth...twenty-fifth...fiftieth anniversaries? What if those members were asked to reflect, in writing or in a conference with the minister, on the significance of their baptisms and these reflections were printed in the newsletter?

Talk of baptism reminds us that Disciples identity includes not only a commitment to freedom but also a commitment, inherent in believers' baptism, to be disciplined followers of Christ (e.g., engaging in daily prayer and Bible study, or using as much of our resources as possible in God's service). Discipline, however, need not only apply to individual Christians. What if elders, in an annual retreat, identified *corporate* disciplines for the congregation to undertake during the coming year? Perhaps prayer for a different country each week, including (especially) those regarded as enemies by our nation...an invitation to a neighboring congregation, perhaps one that is theologically or culturally unlike ours, to cooperative mission or other ecumenical activity...a program of recycling as part of our commitment to protect God's good creation...These shouldn't be seen as options on which the congregation votes. They are corporate practices to which we are rightly called by those we entrust with spiritual leadership.

Restructuring Regions

We will address the need for restructuring regions later in this book, but here we want to observe that councils of churches provide a helpful analogy for understanding the way *The Design* envisions the role and function of regions. Councils, in our experience, are frequently misunderstood as structures alongside the churches rather than as fellowships or communities of the churches themselves. To put it another way, the essence (the "churchly character") of a council of churches is the relationship, the mutual commitment, of the churches to each other, not their relationship to an office in Geneva or New York or Minneapolis. A council is "we," not "they."

In the same way, regions are not structures alongside the congregations or offices that do things on behalf of the congregations. A region, understood theologically, is an expression of covenantal relationship among congregations to be the church together in that place. Thus, a key question for regional life is how congregations manifest this mutual accountability. Are there "marks of commitment," not to "the region" but to *each other as region,* that could be lifted up and regularly reaffirmed in assembly? Imagine that participation in regional life includes a public commitment to pray for other congregations by name and to provide assistance to congregations that need it to carry out mission in their location. The role of regional leadership, then, would be to hold congregations accountable to such commitments. At regional assemblies, instead of a regular role call, congregations might be asked to report on—to give account of—how they have lived out a particular covenantal promise.

Regional oversight of ministry is one area in which mainline denominations have developed obvious structures of accountability—in large part, out of a fear of abusive behavior by clergy. It still isn't clear, however, that ministers are held fully accountable to the declarations they make at ordination. Aren't there, for example, expectations we should have for one another about the practice of collegiality? Regional ministers tell us that regular, widespread participation in clergy retreats helps to develop a common mind among colleagues and to build trust in regional leadership. If so, shouldn't attendance at such retreats be expected of ministers in standing through the region?

Developing a Representative General Assembly

At the "General Church" level, a familiar mantra for Disciples is that the General Assembly speaks to but not for the congregations; but is this really an adequate formulation for a covenantal community? Hasn't our fear of hierarchical structures kept Disciples from developing the General Assembly as a body representative of the whole church? According to *The*

Design, the General Assembly is "to manifest the wholeness and unity of the church" (par. 37). This doesn't simply mean to be an inclusive gathering but to declare, to the best of its ability, the church's wholeness with respect to faith and mission. It is hard not to conclude from *The Design,* writes Disciples theologian Jim Duke, that "the exercise of teaching authority is the assembly's stock in trade."[16]

With this in mind, we would like to see the General Board of the church identify two or three priority issues every two years on which authoritative teaching (i.e., theological guidance) is needed: Should unbaptized children take Communion? What can Christians say, on the basis of the gospel, about policies on immigration? The Board would then invite congregations (perhaps at regional gatherings), seminaries, and general units to participate in the preparation of study documents for action at a near-future General Assembly. The goal in a covenantal community is not to win political victories or to bask in the glow of having been prophetic, but to build up the shared life of the body through the best possible discernment of God's will.

Such a process has been inaugurated with the churchwide study on homosexuality. It removes such issues from a politicized, purely legislative arena, but it should not remove them from action by the Assembly. At some point the church needs to speak its mind, to make public witness. Of course, room is always made for dissent. But when the most representative decision-making body speaks—after careful, churchwide reflection—shouldn't there be a bias in the direction of assent?

All of this assumes, of course, that congregations prepare for General Assemblies with study and prayer. We don't think it is casting aspersions to say that many voting representatives are self-selected ("Who wants to do it this year?") and ill-prepared, which is clearly not adequate if the Assembly is to be a teaching body and a point of accountability. It is also crucial for representatives to report back to their congregations and to invite discussion of the major Assembly actions. The General

Minister and President's "state of the church" address might be edited for video presentation as a starting point for such conversation.

We don't want to be misunderstood. The authors of this book greatly value the historic Disciples commitment to the freedom that is ours in Christ. This is part of our DNA as a movement; without it we would not be Disciples. Beyond that, the reason for our nineteenth-century protest against authoritarian religion has by no means disappeared in the early years of the twenty-first century. Decision-making within the Roman Catholic and Orthodox churches, for example, still strikes most Disciples as overly coercive and hierarchical, giving too much weight to the tradition of corporate teachings and not enough to the dictates of conscience. Disciples will insist—rightly, we believe—that top-down decision-making, while it may create some degree of behavioral conformity, cannot bring about the shared embrace of loyalties that makes for true community. This, as we see it, is part of the Disciples' contribution to ecumenical renewal.

Freeing the Church from Radical Individualism

Disciples ourselves suffer from the opposite problem. If the challenge for reformers within the Roman Catholic Church or the Southern Baptist Convention is to free the individual from the domination of the church, the challenge for us is to free the church from the domination of the individual. We, too, have failed to hold an appropriate tension between personal freedom and interdependent community.

Every church, if it is to be church, must exercise authority. It must, that is, develop ways of making decisions and teaching the faith that (1) ensure the community's identity as a people of the gospel, (2) enable the body to engage faithfully and corporately in mission, and (3) provide guidance for members as they struggle to enact the gospel in their daily lives. A healthy church, as we envision it, will allow, even encourage, the "three d's"—*dialogue, diversity,* and *dissent;* but its members will also recognize that the teachings and decisions of the community have a claim on them.

We can summarize our concerns as follows:

- In the absence of structures of mutual accountability, we are likely to see even greater loss of identity and consequent fragmentation. If the claims of personal perspective or congregational perspective are not brought into dialogue with the authoritative claims of the larger fellowship, then the church is bound to lack direction and cohesion. "Rugged individualism" in the body of Christ means that exercises of power, not discernment, have the upper hand.

- In the absence of authoritative teaching by the church (through authorized curricula, Assembly-approved studies, etc.), such teaching will be increasingly undertaken by individuals or groups that are not necessarily accountable to the total community. Some*one* makes decisions about what the church proclaims or how it worships, and, without a mutually accountable process for doing so, we end up guided more by chance than collective choice. The "Word to the Church on Authority," produced by the Disciples Commission on Theology, is very blunt: "A church which is unwilling to search for a common understanding of Christian authority will be controlled by biblicism, self-seeking individuals, or self-serving institutions."[17]

- Without a deep sense of the mutual accountability that goes with covenant, conflicts will continue to be viewed in us/them, win/lose terms, and church assemblies seen as arenas for political victories rather than theological conversations.

- In the absence of covenantal community, Disciples will be unable to respond effectively to ecumenical initiatives from the universal church. We now realize that an overemphasis on private judgment in matters of faith, once seen as a requirement for unity, actually drives Christians apart.

- In the absence of some sort of communal teaching, the prophetic teaching role of local pastors is likely to be further blunted. As long as pastors are accountable only to the congregation without a body of teaching to which to appeal, we can hardly expect ministers to speak with prophetic authority, no matter how idolatrous the community may become. It is astonishing how many pastors still manage to preach prophetically, but the point is that they are not supported in this by the wider church.

- In the absence of structures and processes of mutual accountability, Disciples will be increasingly unable—as church—to offer clear, confident witness against the false gods of the world. When, in 2003, churches around the world spoke and taught against preemptive war in Iraq, Disciples (despite a great heritage of peacemaking on the part of various leaders) could only contribute a personal letter from the General Minister and President. Do we really have nothing to say (or no way of saying anything) as church about such matters?

We are convinced that despite the cultural trends (or perhaps because of them), Disciples and other Christians are experiencing a deep hunger for interdependent community, for a faith that demands discipline and thus makes a difference in the way we live, for a church that is able to offer bold, even countercultural, witness to society. We are also aware, however, that a covenantal ecclesiology is a very difficult way of being church. To demonstrate disciplined community that yet values diversity, dialogue, and dissent—to model responsible freedom—requires real spiritual maturity. But if we Disciples don't act as a covenantal people, then we become, in effect, clubs of culturally formed individuals, preoccupied with "the relief of psychic distress and institutional maintenance."[18] We become useless in the divine struggle against powers and principalities, unable to name and confront the idolatries of our time and place because we are they.

CHAPTER 3

Scripture

Common Source, Diverse Readers

"The Bible is to the intellectual and moral world of [humanity]," wrote Alexander Campbell, "what the sun is to the planets in our system—the fountain and source of light and life, spiritual and eternal."[1] His view set the direction for the way Disciples revere and approach scripture. As all other Protestants, we are "people of the book," having rejected papal authority and church tradition for the "paper pope." But the singular place biblical authority has had in our common life has placed special demands on Disciples. As Disciples New Testament scholar Eugene Boring observes, "Disciples have always assumed or affirmed that the content of the faith is identical with or inseparable from the message of the Bible. This centrality of the Bible for articulating the meaning of faith is especially crucial for a denomination that has distanced itself from creeds and tradition."[2]

Disciples Interpreting Scripture

Boring's book *Disciples and the Bible* is the most definitive history of Disciples interpretation of scripture to date. He divides this history of biblical interpretation into five generations based on the primary Disciples biblical scholars in each generation. This is an important study that the authors of this book need not repeat. But we do want to bring special focus to something Boring discusses briefly near the end his book, something we consider the primary challenge facing Disciples today, and we also want to suggest a response different from the one he offers.[3] This challenge is the need for us to reclaim the authority of scripture for our life together, a need that is urgent—not least because for most Disciples laity and more than a few clergy, biblical authority seems to have no real meaning or is bound to a biblical literalism that contradicts the history Boring discusses. Speaking where scripture speaks and remaining silent where scripture is silent may have expressed a genuine desire to submit ourselves to the authority of the Bible, but we have never been able to put that desire effectively into practice. This is the case for several reasons.

Pervasive Biblical Illiteracy

One reason is a pervasive biblical illiteracy among Disciples that almost every pastor confronts, and that Boring says began to emerge in the fourth generation of our movement. Noting the contrast with earlier Disciples, he writes, "As one reads the works and personal letters of the first three generations of Disciples, one cannot help but be struck by how well they knew the content of the Bible. They not only knew isolated verse and stories; they knew the story line as a whole, and formed the framework for their own life's story."[4] This is certainly not a level of biblical knowledge found among church members today. Disciples are not unique in this regard, but that is of little consolation as we struggle to find common ground for who speaks for Disciples. Millions of Christians simply do not know what the Bible says, and Disciples are among them.

Mixed Understandings

A second factor that immediately complicated the effort of our founders to draw exclusively on the Bible as their authority was the mixed message they conveyed about understanding it. On the one hand they talked about a "simple gospel," but in the next breath provided a process for interpretation that was anything but simple. Not only did Alexander Campbell say, "The words and sentences of the Bible are to be translated, interpreted, and understood according to the same code of laws and principles of interpretation by which other ancient writing are translated and understood,"[5] he enumerated seven steps for biblical interpretation[6] he believed would achieve this goal. These steps make understanding the gospel anything but simple.

Searching to know the historical circumstances of a book (who the author was, why the book was written); distinguishing between what is commanded, promised, or taught through a thorough study of the book's language; considering the dominant usage of particular words to understand their meaning—these hardly suggest that the Bible's message is one the average church member can quickly comprehend. If interpreting the Bible is a task that belongs to the whole church (meaning the universal church) and needs to be "rational, critical, and scholarly," as Campbell and others insisted,[7] it seems to us that Boring is correct in his assessment: "The simple gospel, in contrast to 'human speculation,' became a buzz word for all later Disciples history until the present day. [But] the term 'simple' has not been an unmixed blessing in Disciples efforts to articulate the Christian faith."[8]

At the same time, though, as essential and invaluable as Disciples have believed historical criticism is in understanding the biblical message, the question with which we continue to struggle is the nature of the authority of the Bible when its texts are subject to such varied interpretations. Some among us, such as the dissident group Disciples Heritage Fellowship, believe the answer is for Disciples to embrace biblical literalism. In 1989 this group's leaders brought a resolution to the floor of the General Assembly that would have declared the Bible as the sole authority for Disciples in a way that would have been a de facto affirmation of the inerrancy of scripture. The Assembly wisely rejected the resolution because of its implicit assault on historical criticism, which Disciples believe is an aid to understanding the Bible. The reality of Disciples church life today is that even though there may be ministers and church members who are biblical literalists, this is not the way the majority of Disciples clergy and laity think about the Bible.

That said, however, an unintended consequence of the widespread acceptance of historical criticism has been the growth of specialization in biblical studies, which, as Boring observes, has created the impression that "responsible biblical interpretation is more technical than it is and/or that it is beyond the competence of an 'ordinary' church member."[9] This attitude is evident in the bifurcation of what is taught to ministers in seminary and what is taught to laity in the church. The chasm between the two is so wide that one doesn't seem to be on speaking terms with the other. Sunday school classes and, in many instances, Bible courses taught by clergy seldom venture into higher criticism that could inform the way laypeople understand texts. We think this sells Disciples laity short. In fact, we think that—in numbers larger than some might suppose—Disciples laity want the kind of help in understanding the Bible higher historical criticism provides. They are no less rational or critical thinkers than clergy. What they lack is the training in the skills of modern hermeneutics. If the *perception* is that biblical interpretation is beyond the competence of "ordinary" church members, as Borings suggests, this does not mean biblical interpretation *does require* a level of interpretative skills most laypeople do not possess. The issue is not competence, but the lack of specific knowledge that can be acquired.

This is a problem congregational pastors can correct, except that too many of them suffer from it as well. Not having language skills to read Hebrew and Greek for themselves, and finding the demands of congregational, regional, and general church ministry time-consuming, keeping up with biblical scholarship has become more than many are able to do. We also think this has contributed to the decline in Bible studies taught by ministers. Lacking confidence in what has been happening in the field of biblical studies, and being reluctant to put themselves in the position of having to answer questions about troublesome texts (Lev. 20:18 on homosexuality and Jn. 14:6 that suggests Jesus is the only means of salvation are examples), pastors often avoid teaching the Bible as they were taught it.

In this kind of church culture, biblical authority will inevitably be more words than practice until we make a conscious effort to change it. While the authors of this book believe the 1989 General Assembly was right in rejecting the resolution on the Bible, we also think the level of support for the resolution (the vote was nearly split) suggests the issue of biblical authority was—and remains—a serious concern for many Disciples pastors and congregations and has not yet been addressed adequately. Given the turbulent times we have been experiencing in which we have seemed to lack both a clear sense of identity and direction as a church, the time is ripe for Disciples to renew our commitment to the authority of scripture.

Reaffirming Scriptural Authority

We understand that the reasons for the erosion of biblical authority are multiple and complex, but it may also be the case that a reaffirmation of scriptural authority is not as difficult as it appears. In fact, it may be a matter of stating the obvious. What we are suggesting is that the key to Disciples reclaiming biblical authority is for us as a church to embrace that which the church has long said were its four sources of authority: what is known as the "Wesleyan Quadrilateral." We believe this approach holds more promise than Boring's two alternate proposals, neither of which strikes us as very helpful to laity.[10]

The "Wesleyan Quadrilateral" is actually a phrase first used by Albert Outler,[11] an American theologian who in 1964 described the four primary sources of authority used by John

Wesley, the eighteenth-century founder of the Methodist Church. They were (1) scripture, (2) tradition, (3) reason, and (4) experience. Outler himself later said in his book on Wesley that he regretted using the phrase, "Wesleyan Quadrilateral," because it implied that Wesley considered these four sources equal, when in fact he did not. Wesley believed scripture was the primary source, and the other three derived from it.

Centrality of Scripture

Our position is more nuanced than Wesley's, yet, we would argue, still affirms the centrality of scripture in Disciples life. We prefer to say that scripture is the first among equals in the context of the Quadrilateral. The Bible is the authority to which we have always made an appeal in times of controversy or debate, but this trustworthiness of the authority of scripture depends on the interplay between tradition, reason, and experience as it is interpreted. Each in its own way enhances our understanding of the biblical message. This is as it should be, since each plays a decisive role in the way all humans interpret the world. Wesley believed scripture was the primary authority because he assumed that the biblical message was self-explanatory. That is, texts unveil their meaning to all who seek truth, and different texts can be used to illuminate one another.

Human Reasoning

As we have already seen, our own leaders discovered that this approach to the Bible fell short of its claim. Reliable interpretations of the Bible need the best in human reasoning to enhance their credibility and trustworthiness. The best of our early leaders understood that there is no conflict between faith and reason when both are properly understood. Jesus invited us to love God with all our minds as well as hearts and souls (Mt. 22:37). The human mind is a gift that is to be used to help us grow in maturity of faith and trust in God. What we are saying is that a conscious reaffirmation of the primacy of scripture in

Disciples life will necessarily also affirm our heritage as good thinkers who use our minds to understand the Bible.

Personal Experience

The same is true for human experience. Every Disciples church member is a walking interpretive context. We bring all our personal experiences into the conversation with scripture. What we hear and how we hear it are shaped by the totality of those experiences that have made us who we are. To illustrate, several sub-groups of a larger gathering of Disciples laity were discussing their images of God. One group put "Father" as their most dominant image. The leader asked them to share with the others why they did so. They responded that "God as Father" was an image that had grown out of their consistent experiences of growing up with a wonderful father figure in the home. The leader then asked how they thought this image might impact people whose experience of "father" had not been positive, and in fact might have been traumatic. The group had not thought about it at all. Nor had they made the connection between their personal experience and their image of God.

Experience is an inevitable influence on the way we read the Bible. If anything, in fact, the danger is that is has become the only source to which many people make appeal, consciously or unconsciously, as they make decisions. Yet it is a factor that cannot be ignored by the church in how its words about matters of faith are perceived or heard. Just as only 4 percent of American Catholics follow the teachings of their church on birth control,[12] so Disciples must be aware of a similar impact of personal experience on what *we say* the *Bible* teaches.

Church Tradition

Church tradition, which is also part of the Wesleyan Quadrilateral, is perhaps the source of authority Disciples seem most reluctant to acknowledge. Yet it is consistent with our historical commitment to being part of the whole church rather than living in a world unto ourselves. Boring skillfully documents the fact that Disciples in every generation have sought to understand the Bible in an ecumenical context, even as the meaning of that context has changed through the years. The first three generations of Disciples believed that studying the Bible would produce a simple and clear understanding of the gospel and the church, which would draw all Christians together. As it became obvious to later generations that there was no single "pattern" for the one church in scripture, the meaning of the ecumenical context changed:

> To have the ecumenical orientation is the Disciple tradition. In ecumenical dialogue, we have come to express our conviction that we belong to the whole church by statements such as, "We interpret for ourselves, but not by ourselves." Concretely, this means the use of ecumenical resources in interpreting the Bible. This needs to be distinguished from the style of resources that claims to be "nondenominational" in the sense of a-theological. Disciples pastor-teachers need to look for ecumenical commentaries and theological resources, not merely lowest-common-denominator secularized nontheological ones. Concretely, this ecumenical perspective also means incorporating the sense of the church's whole tradition (including the ecumenical creeds) as the guide and context for our encounter with the Bible.[13]

What Boring says is not only a strong affirmation of the role of tradition in how Disciples work with scripture as our primary authority; it also underscores the place of reason and experience as being supportive of this need. Each not only contributes to the other three, but together they bring credibility to our claim to be a church that considers the Bible our authority. In the context of America today, such a claim is often met with suspicion by people wary of religious efforts to impose beliefs and morals on everyone else. On the other hand, it is possible that they will not be put off at all by an appeal to scriptural authority in a church that promotes the right and responsibility of Christians to think for themselves on matters of faith and morals.

Reaffirming the Inspiration of Scripture

One of the important benefits to reestablishing the authority of the Bible within the context of the Wesleyan Quadrilateral among Disciples is that it also reaffirms our commitment to the inspiration of scripture. Unfortunately, biblical inspiration has been misused by some Christians to argue for inerrancy and infallibility. The text they most often cite is 2 Timothy 3:16–17, which reads, "All scripture is inspired by God and is useful for teaching, for reproof, for correction, and for training in righteousness, so that everyone who belongs to God may be proficient, equipped for every good work." But the meaning of the word for "inspired" in this text has no relationship to inerrancy or infallibility. The meaning of the word is "breathe." The Hebrews writer is saying that scripture has been "breathed into," just as human life sprang from the "breath" of God.

According to Genesis, human beings were given life when God "breathed into" them and they became living creatures (2:7). Further, the concept of God "breathing" life into the whole of creation goes back to the origin of the name "YHWH" itself. The name cannot be pronounced since it has no vowels in the Hebrew. It can only be "breathed" and is generally translated as "Lord." Rabbi Arthur Waskow says that because the name is unpronounceable, the more appropriate meaning is "Breath of Life" or "Breathing Life of the World." As he puts it, "God breathes us. We breathe God."[14]

This is how we can interpret the inspiration of scripture. God "breathed" it, and we "breathe" in the words that become the word of life for us. In this way we can affirm that all scripture is inspired because we experience the "breath" of God that assures us that God is present in both the words of the text and our effort to understand them. This meaning of inspiration saves us from the distraction of arguing about inerrancy and infallibility that diminishes the authority of the Bible by attaching human concepts to it that find no support in scripture itself.

Reclaiming Obedience

One other dimension to reaffirming the authority of the Bible in the context of the Wesleyan Quadrilateral is that it opens the door to Disciples also reclaiming the use of the word *obedience*. Given the abuse of power both state and church have demonstrated through the centuries and the experience many people have with such abuse in personal relationships, it is no surprise that the word *obedience* does not illicit a positive reaction. Yet its Latin root has nothing to do with the use or abuse of power. It comes from the root "to listen." Therefore, to call Disciples to obedience to the authority of the Bible in the context of tradition, reason, and experience means that as a community of faith we can "listen" to scripture as we are given minds and hearts to understand it.

Further, the listening should be done in community. More specifically, it should be done in covenant. Not much of what we have been saying about the authority of scripture for Disciples will matter unless it exists within a community that is committed to a covenantal life as we discussed in the previous chapter. Disciples have labored to balance authority and freedom of thought in the way we have approached the Bible. This has naturally produced different interpretations of what the Bible says and how it is to be used, especially in regard to difficult contemporary issues such as war, poverty, abortion, homosexuality, and others. Just as our founders realized that the unity of the church could not be based on general assent to creedal statements, we will not maintain a sense of oneness as a church through a common view of biblical texts. This leaves the hope for unity in the midst of diverse interpretation dependent upon a covenantal commitment to be one church.

Covenant of the Heart

The church practices a peculiar kind of covenant, one of the heart. The key to this covenant of the heart is an appropriate pride about our life together. Though it sounds a bit like an oxymoron, perhaps the phrase is "a humble pride," the kind of pride that is born of differentiation similar to that experienced in families. Differentiation based on family identity is not "over against" other families. It is "alongside" them, a healthy differentiation that creates an appropriate pride without denigrating another. It seems to us that "family" is a better description of who we are as a church than any other label we can use, certainly one better suited to our heart as a people than "denomination" ever has been. We have a common ancestry and heritage of which we ought to be proud. Disciples have never needed theological agreement to experience a oneness known to families. In this way we have been a beacon of light in a world torn apart by bitter divisions that separate families, neighbors, and nations.

This is a covenant made possible by a keen awareness that the only thing that can and does hold us one to the other is the person of Jesus Christ. We belong to one another, as Bonhoeffer said, because we first belong to him. The authors of this book believe that because Disciples have no creed but Christ and no ecclesial system of authority but the practice of equality between clergy and laity in ministry, we have been shaped by this one spirit in a way that makes covenant possible. To use a biblical metaphor, we have eaten the scroll whose words have given spirit to our life together. What is more, at times we have shown an amazing capacity to arrive at the same interpretative destination as a result. The centrality of weekly Communion, the practice of believer's baptism by immersion, our early embrace—at least in principle—of the role of women in ordained ministry, our steadfast opposition to the scandal of a divided church, and our commitment to racial justice within the life of our own church as well as the life of the nation are encouraging examples of how Disciples can speak with one voice.

They also suggest that the kind of covenant of the heart we are underscoring is not one we have to create. It is one we simply need to remember. When we do, we will be able to sit together at the table of biblical interpretation and discuss and debate the words of the Bible that will speak the words of life to us as a people joined in discipleship.[15] This will free us to use scripture not as a sword to strike at one another or others when disagreement arises, but as the common authority to which all of us make appeal as we discern together the truth Jesus promised would set us free (Jn. 8:32).

What is most distinctive about the Christian Church (Disciples of Christ) is that we look to scripture for guidance and embrace one another in covenant because we belong to Jesus Christ first. Covenant and scripture are the foundation for Disciples life, and will determine in the days ahead the kind of church we will become as we adapt to ever-changing circumstances and challenges.

CHAPTER 4

The Lord's Supper

One Table, Many Guests

Disciples identity has remained remarkably stable even as our practices have been constantly evolving. This is clearly evident in how we understand the meaning of the Lord's Supper, which continues to be core to Disciples worship. Though Disciples historians debate whether or not a sacramental interpretation of Communion is or is not alien to the understanding of our founders on the subject, all agree that Communion as an act of remembrance has been a dominant interpretation.[1] More than that, weekly observance of the Lord's Supper and baptism by immersion are the enduring and distinguishing practices of our denomination. As the Vision Team statement declares: "As part of the one body of Christ, we welcome all to the Lord's Table as God has welcomed us."[2]

The Lord's Supper as Identity-giving

Being "people of the table" is more than a slogan for us, and the chalice is more than a denominational symbol. Both underscore the fact that the Lord's Supper identifies something very basic about who we are as a community of faith. We are a people for whom no worship is complete without Communion, not least because coming to the Lord's table is a moment when we consciously seek to embody the oneness of the church to which we have witnessed from the beginning.

The Lord's Supper played a decisive role in the birth of both the Christians of Kentucky led by Barton W. Stone and the Disciples of Pennsylvania led by Thomas and Alexander Campbell. The common bond that played no small role in their merger in 1832 was a passion for the unity of the one church of Christ on earth coming around the one table with one loaf. Stone had envisioned a public Communion service being a great Christian witness when he called for it to be held the first week in August, 1801, at the Cane Ridge Meeting House. The gathering exploded into a revival meeting that was the catalyst for the Second Great Awakening on the American frontier and the eventual birth of the Christians of Kentucky movement.

While we do not know if those gathered at Cane Ridge recognized in the experience that denominationalism stood over against the prayer of Jesus "that they may all be one" (Jn. 17:21), we do know that within three years the unity of the church had become their passion. Thus, on June 28, 1804, six former Presbyterian ministers, including Stone, witnessed the *Last Will and Testament* of the Springfield Presbytery that they had formed after Cane Ridge, and vowed to wear the name "Christian" as a sign of their shared allegiance to Jesus Christ and him only.

Five years later another gathering around the Lord's table led Thomas Campbell to choose the oneness of the church represented by the Lord's Supper over the barriers that existed within the Presbyterian Church at that time. So from the beginning, gathering around the Lord's table has sparked a passion among us for the oneness of the church in the face of theological barriers between and within denominations that divide the body of Christ.

The Lord's Supper and Church Unity

This oneness of the church lies at the core of why Communion expresses our identity as the Christian Church (Disciples of Christ) more than anything else we do together. Among the seven propositions Alexander Campbell used to describe the meaning of what he preferred to call "the breaking of the loaf,"[3] there being one loaf representing the one body of Christ with many members was paramount: "As there is but one literal body, and one mystical or figurative body having many members, so there must be but one loaf."[4] Barton W. Stone had a similar view of the importance of the one loaf being broken at the "Table of the Lord."[5]

As Christians share the loaf one with another, wrote Campbell, this was the equivalent of them saying to each other, "You, my brother [or sister], once an alien, are now a citizen of heaven; once a stranger are now brought home to the family of God."[6] Thus, Campbell affirmed what the apostle Paul had already said, that the one table and one loaf symbolize the oneness of the church as the community under Christ (Eph. 4:1–6). The Lord's Supper was for him so much more than a ritual. He believed that as long as those who partake are conscious of its meaning, it functions as the glue that holds the household of God together. From our formation, then, coming to the Lord's table has never been a passive act for Disciples, but a moment when, in the action of eating the "bread of life," we participate in the oneness of the church of Christ on earth.

This understanding of life around the Lord's table explains why unity is not tangential to the meaning of this table in the Disciples tradition. It is central, born of the fact that it does not belong to us. It is the *Lord's* table. We come at God's invitation, which is why Disciples say that we neither invite anyone to nor debar them from the table. It is not ours. It is the Lord's. When the church claims ownership, the table represents division. When it remembers that the table belongs to God, the table becomes the gathering place for the one community under Christ.

Freedom to Preside at the Table

Unity was also why Campbell insisted that any Christian can preside at the Lord's table. "All Christians are members of the family or house of God," he wrote, and, thus, "are called and constituted a royal and holy priesthood."[7] This understanding of unity is also a part of our identity. Anyone, Campbell said, may "bless God for the Lord's table, its loaf and cup, and approach it without fear."[8] This was not a unity of human origin. It was born of the relationship Christians have one to the other by virtue of belonging to Jesus Christ. Campbell believed that the oneness Christians share with one another was the by-product of the bread and cup being commemorative of Jesus' death on the cross. "Ties that spring from eternal love," he wrote, "revealed in blood, and addressed to his senses, draw forth all that is within [Christians] of complacent affection and feeling to those joint heirs with [them] of the grace of eternal life."[9] Campbell, therefore, quotes the old chorus, "Bless be the tie that binds our hearts in Christian love."[10]

The Supper as the Heart of Christian Worship

The oneness of the body of Christ symbolized by the love of God to which the Lord's Supper points is why celebrating it at "every stated meeting" of the church was the "capital proposition" on which Campbell was most insistent. He believed that everything else about "the breaking of the loaf" was preliminary to this purpose. Observance at every gathering was essential to the nurture of the moral health of the Christian community.[11] From what he said about it, it is clear that for Campbell what the Lord's Supper represented made it the heart of Christian worship. Though the supper is not an end in itself, it *is* a symbol of divine love that redeems and unites all those who gather in the name of Jesus to break bread and share the cup.

What is particularly noteworthy about Campbell's understanding of the Lord's Supper was that he obviously believed the effect of partaking of it was more rational than spiritual. This is not to say he rejected the presence of the Holy Spirit in the act of Communion. Disciples historian Mark Toulouse says Campbell believed Christian character was enhanced by the Holy Spirit working through the symbols of bread and wine.[12] Even at that, it is clear from Campbell's own hand that he was confident the impact of the Holy Spirit would be seen in and through further understanding of the meaning of Communion. "Every time the disciples assemble around the Lord's table," he wrote, "they are furnished with a new argument also against sin, as well as with a new proof of the love of God."[13]

Both of these were fruits of a mind that understood the meaning of this institution of the church. Campbell affirmed the bread and the cup as symbols of an act of God, and the institution of the Lord's Supper itself as one no person other than Jesus could have so established.[14] Still, being the rationalist he was, Campbell said nothing about the effect of the community breaking bread together to suggest its effect was other than a renewal of understanding and attitude.

The Supper as Symbol

This is in part why Disciples have struggled with the concept of Communion as a "sacrament" of the church, a "means of grace." We are a people for whom the bread and the cup have always served as emblems, symbols, that remind us of the gift of salvation in Jesus Christ, a meaning plainly discernable for the thoughtful Christian. Thus, we are heirs of the Protestant reformers who rejected transubstantiation (the priestly act of consecration in which the bread and wine become the body and blood of Jesus). Nor did our founders focus much on the alternative, consubstantiation, or the belief that the presence of Christ is experienced in the act of partaking of the bread and cup, not in the emblems themselves. They did not speak of the Lord's Supper with this kind of language.

Remembering as Representation

In most Disciples congregations today the language surrounding the Lord's Supper reflects the view that it is an act in which the church remembers the sacrifice Jesus made on our behalf. Seldom do the prayers of elders make reference to the manifest presence of the raised Christ in the act of breaking bread or drinking wine, and certainly never that the bread and cup become the body and blood of Christ. The language and meaning of Communion for Disciples more often than not underscores the rational approach to the Lord's table that is Campbell's legacy. It is a memorial meal that reminds the church of Christ's sacrifice and our call to follow his example.

At the same time, some among us believe the Disciples ecumenical commitment has helped to move us beyond this predominantly rational view to the point of claiming the church's larger understanding of the biblical meaning of "remembrance."[15] In its 1991 "Word of the Church on *The Lord's Supper*," the Commission on Theology, a working group of the Council of Christian Unity, summarized the ecumenical consensus:

> As Paul recounts the tradition known to him, he speaks of remembrance: "This do in remembrance of me" (1 Cor. 11:23–26). The Greek term used here, *anamnesis*, certainly involves memory, but it carries special force. It is not merely a recollection of something long gone and hence remote from us, but a re-presentation which makes what is past a vivid and lively reality here and now. Jesus Christ himself with all he has accomplished for us and for all creation is present in the *anamnesis*.
>
> In remembering as *anamnesis* we go beyond thinking of an event that took place in bygone days. Through this joyful celebration God's saving acts and promises in Jesus Christ are re-called from the past; they are brought before our hearts and minds with stark immediacy. A Spiritual coming down from black Christian tradition captures this meaning well: in asking "were you there when they crucified my Lord," the answer "yes" is already given.[16]

Certainly memory functioned in the life of the early Christians in the act of Communion in a way not embraced by many Disciples congregations. In his seminal work *Jesus in the Memory of the Early Church*,[17] Nils Dahl explores how "anamnesis" was more than a recalling of a past event in both Israel and the church. It was, he says, much more than the church preserving an image of Jesus. Instead, the first Christians let their memory of him form their thoughts and actions.[18] Thus, Dahl contends, Christians in every generation remember Jesus because we already live in him, having been baptized, committing ourselves to him, and now gathering around his table. The Lord's Supper, he says, was central to the church's act of remembering, not as an individual experience as Disciples tend to make it, but as a moment in worship when the church as the body of Christ enters into collective experience in recalling the history of salvation. The Lord's Supper was in effect this history "re-presented by the sacramental commemoration."[19]

We can see, then, that when the apostle Paul writes that Jesus instituted the Lord's Supper with the words, "Do this in remembrance of me" (1 Cor. 11:24), this power of memory to engage those gathered to experience the suffering and death of Jesus is what Paul had in mind. From this perspective, far from being benign, the act of remembrance was to enter into an experience in which the past and the present become as one. Paul was, of course, reflecting a Jewish understanding of memory in these words. In the Torah remembering was a means of bringing a past event into the present in such a way that those who were remembering began to participate in the event itself, as, for example:

> A wandering Aramean was my ancestor; he went down into Egypt and lived there as an alien, few in number, and there he became a great nation, mighty and populous. When the Egyptians treated us harshly and afflicted us, by imposing hard labor on us, we cried to the LORD, the God of our ancestors; the LORD heard

our voice and saw our affliction, our toil, and our oppression. The LORD brought us out of Egypt with a mighty hand and an outstretched arm, with a terrifying display of power, and with signs and wonders; and he brought us into this place and gave us this land, a land flowing with milk and honey. (Deut. 26:5b–9)

In the text itself, as the community tells its story, it begins to participate personally and collectively in the story. The pronoun "he" becomes "us," and the gathered community begins to experience the past suffering and rescue. It was only natural, then, that the first Christians would carry this understanding of the function and power of memory into their celebration of the Lord's Supper.

The Supper and the Holy Spirit

Throughout our history Disciples have been a people who claimed to come to the Lord's table as an act of remembrance. But we may well have allowed the rational dimension of Communion to overshadow the power of memory to shape us as it was understood to do by the first Christians. If so, we have overlooked what Barton W. Stone believed about the work of the Holy Spirit as the Spirit of Christ himself working in a Christian's life:

It is the spirit of holiness, which, when received, hungers and thirsts for righteousness, pants for God and a perfect conformity to his lovely character. It is the spirit of adoption, *whereby we cry Abba, Father.* It is the spirit of love to God, and man. It is the spirit which unites the whole family of God. It is the spirit of power, by which we are enabled to oppose successfully every temptation, and every enemy. It is the spirit of liberty, not of bondage; *for where the spirit of the Lord is, there is liberty.* In a word, it is the spirit, the fruits of which are *love, joy, peace, long suffering, gentleness, goodness, faithfulness, meekness, and temperance.* Gal. v. 22, 23.[20]

Stone was, of course, a rationalist himself, but his emphasis on the work of the Holy Spirit highlighted the mystical side of faith that Campbell's rationalism did not. Were we to reclaim the Stone emphasis on the Holy Spirit, coming to the table of remembrance might be deepened considerably so that we not only "think" about being one in Christ around the Lord's table, but actually experience it by means of memory.

Thus, we open ourselves to a greater appreciation for the mystical dimension of the Lord's Supper that doesn't contradict the rational value of it, but transcends it. Unity around the table can never be solely a fruit of understanding. Human fallibility, something Stone was very much aware of, always undercuts our best intentions. The Holy Spirit is in the end the power for creating oneness in the body of Christ. Our minds can hinder or help in this process, but it is finally an experience, not simply an understanding.[21]

The Supper and the Christian Life

The same is true for leaving the Lord's table as a community committed to the cross—not only serving as a symbol of salvation, but also a sign of the life we are willing to live. If remembering Jesus at the table is intended to shape and form us to live as he lived, or, "to live our lives the way he would live them, if he were us,"[22] then the Lord's Supper calls us together and sends us out as one people. This is what our founders understood as the rightful response of faith to the grace of God. God's action and our response of faith are inseparable. For Disciples grace and works go hand in hand. While the response of faith varies among Disciples, historically we have understood that unity and justice seeking together constitute the *ne plus ultra,* or highest quality, of human response to God's initiative.

In an age when faith is often thought to be individualistic and even private, remembering that Communion and the response of faith are inseparable can serve to call us to renew our commitment as a church to unity and justice-seeking. This is especially relevant at a time when Disciples Home Missions no longer has a church and society division, and the bringing of controversial topics to the floor of the General Assembly is discouraged. Can a church that claims the Lord's Supper stands at the center of its worship accept a diminished passion for the oneness of the church or leave justice-seeking to individual conscience and be true to itself?

The Lord's Supper and Disciples' Future

Only the future will tell us the answer, but Disciples history would suggest that all of us should pray for the rekindling of a passion for unity and justice as Disciples come to the table weekly. We have at various points in our past allowed controversy over Communion practices to become more important than its meaning. Should we take by intinction or pass plates through the pews? Should laity administer the meal without clergy involvement? Should unbaptized children be allowed to take Communion, and is it a decision left to parents or one determined by congregation policy? These are not unimportant questions, but neither are they primary ones in any discussion of the Lord's Supper.[23] In the final analysis, what matters is the kind of people we are when we come to the table, and the kind of people this regular experience of the living Christ coming to us in the breaking of bread makes us into over time. An experience of a clergy colleague underscores this point.

He was participating in a worship service of various Disciples congregations that concluded with the celebration of the Lord's Supper. The gathered community was invited to receive the bread and cup by intinction, each person once served turning to offer the bread and cup to the next person in line. After receiving the bread and cup himself, our colleague turned to serve the person standing behind him. When he did, he found himself looking into the eyes of a man who in anger had left the congregation the minister served two years earlier. Both paused, as if unsure of what to do. Our colleague decided to do what he was supposed to, so he repeated the words of Jesus, "This is my body, broken for you; this is my blood, shed for you," and extended the bread and cup to the man. Then he added, "And being at this table together at this moment is more important than anything else that has happened between us."

We believe our founders would say that this is the true meaning and power of the Lord's Supper. Can the same be said of us, or has the Lord's table lost its capacity to impact our collective life? One of the signs that this is at least a possibility is the fact that in the modern era Disciples have followed the Protestant focus on preaching during weekly worship. We have been blessed with pulpit voices past and present that have played, and play now, an essential role in the equipping of church members for living the Christian life in the modern world. But our tradition says that the reason we worship is to break the loaf. Preaching was no small factor in the revival that broke out at Cane Ridge, but the purpose of the meeting in the first place was to publicly celebrate the Lord's Supper. This is a good reminder to the heirs of the Christians of Kentucky that coming to the Lord's table is why we gather in worship. This is why small and/or yoked congregations without clergy present every week worship nonetheless—for the singular purpose of having Communion.

This is what Disciples do. We join together in worship that revolves around Communion. The impact of the sermon on the congregation waxes and wanes from week to week, but the power of the Lord's Supper to remind us of who we are and what we are to do remains constant as long as we come to the table expecting to experience the presence of Christ himself as we break bread together as his disciples. Moreover, being conscious of the power of the table is how we have always avoided the tendency for the act of Communion to become habitual. Familiarity may not breed contempt, but human frailty being what it is, familiarity can certainly lead to a diminished appreciation for what something or someone means to us. Married love can grow cold. Parents can be taken for granted. Friendships can be neglected. Worship can become optional.

The Lord's Supper can become something done without a keen awareness of what it means. It's all a part of the human condition. A universal experience among Disciples occurs when circumstances prevent us from breaking the loaf in a community of faith for a long period of time. Then we experience deep inside what this act truly means to us. Its absence makes us appreciate the gift of the presence of Christ experienced around the table. Nothing indicates that partaking of the Lord's Supper less frequently would make us less vulnerable to it becoming simply an unconscious habit. What is out of sight is often out of mind as well. The challenge is to maintain a keen sense of the significance of what we are doing when we come to the Lord's table.

The same can be said of living the unity and doing justice as ministries to which we believe the table calls us. Experiencing what Communion means is strengthened by living what it means. A fractured community will not be united around the table unless some of those gathered already recognize and are ready to confess the stubborn spirit within them that stands in the way of healing. The Spirit of God can work in mighty ways, but its effect is seldom felt by anyone who is determined to follow his own way or nurse her own wound. The same can be said about the mission of justice-seeking that the table represents. If the community shows little commitment to justice within its own life and in the world, the Lord's Supper is not likely to inspire it to take up this imperative. A Damascus Road experience around the table cannot be ruled out, but our experience is that it seldom happens. The colleague we mentioned at the outset and the man who left his congregation in anger would eventually come to truly reconcile because of how they acted toward one another after they had shared the bread and cup.

To a significant degree worship itself is the celebration of the lived commitment of the community outside the hour of worship. Faithful living is preparation for experiencing unity and the call to justice. Which also means that a divided congregation or one that is tone deaf to the cries of injustice will find it difficult to experience the full measure of the unity and justice Communion represents.

Ultimately, we are pointing to the fact that the Lord's Supper does not exist in a vacuum. To experience the presence of Jesus through the act of remembering is to commit ourselves to living the way he lived, loving the way he loved, serving the way he served. To live this way shows that we have truly remembered. Anything less turns Communion into an empty ritual. For this reason the gospel of John may describe that portion of the Passover Disciples generally ignore, but which may be the most telling in regard to the meaning of Communion for all Christians. It is the story of Jesus washing the feet of the disciples.

While none of the gospels makes reference to Jesus telling the disciples to observe "the breaking of the loaf," John's gospel says that Jesus knelt before his disciples and washed their feet. When Peter protested, Jesus told him he could not be counted as one of his unless he allowed Jesus to perform this act of humility. Afterward John says Jesus instructed the disciples to repeat this act among themselves: "After he had washed their feet, had put on his robe, and had returned to the table, he said to them, 'Do you know what I have done to you? You call me Teacher and Lord—and you are right, for that is what I am. So if I, your Lord and Teacher, have washed your feet, you also ought to wash one another's feet'" (Jn. 13:12–14).

Foot washing has not been a practice used by many Disciples congregations, and then only on rare occasions. But those among us who have experienced foot washing understand that it is a ritual that holds great potential for our experiencing the presence of Christ in a way that breaks our resistance to the full meaning of coming to the table. To kneel before another Christian and wash his or her feet envelops both persons in a sacred moment that says as much as any words we can repeat at the table in regard to why we gather. We are united by a recognition that the breaking of bread and sharing the cup can be no other than the gift of the Spirit of Christ before whom we kneel. To wash the feet of another is to experience the power of what it means to minister to "the least of these who are members of my family" (Mt. 25:40). It may be that the single greatest danger Disciples face as we come to the Lord's table is to underestimate the significance of what we are doing.

CHAPTER 5

Baptism

Bold Discipleship and Humble Spirit

A new ecumenical consensus has emerged over the past half century with regard to the meaning and practice of baptism. Churches still baptize in different ways, but these differences are increasingly seen as enriching rather than dividing—at least for churches involved in the ecumenical movement. The theological consensus of the Consultation on Church Union (now Churches Uniting in Christ) is representative of where things stand:

> Diversity of baptismal practice in the churches reflects different dimensions of the meaning of Baptism into the body of the one Lord. It is therefore appropriate that alternative practices be maintained within a [future united church]. Infant Baptism calls attention to human need and helplessness, and to the reality of God's gracious initiative and action on our behalf. Baptism of confessing believers emphasizes the personal response to grace and the forgiveness of sin. It bears witness to the Church as a community reborn in the Spirit.[1]

Baptism and Ecumenism

This theological shift has certainly affected the Disciples. For generations, members of the Stone-Campbell Movement battled over whether the "pious unimmersed" were Christians and, consequently, whether they might be admitted to membership in our congregations. Thankfully, these controversies are, for the most part, behind us, and we are free to focus on meaning more than mode. To put it another way, what baptism signifies about new life in Christ is far more important than the age of the candidate or the amount of water used. Disciples affirm the immersion of believers as our normative practice for reasons we will emphasize later in this chapter; but we no longer regard this form as so essential that our unity with Christians who practice infant baptism is denied or threatened.

With the end of these battles, Disciples seem to have lost a sense that baptism is crucial to who we are—as if only that which is controversial can be important. It is striking to us, for example, how seldom these days Disciples talk about baptism. Stephen England could still declare in 1963, "Disciples of Christ have been noted for 'majoring in baptism,'"[2] but a scan of the past twenty years of *The Disciple* and *DisciplesWorld* turned up very few articles on the subject. It once was commonplace, say older friends, to hear lengthy references to baptism from Disciples pulpits or at Disciples conventions, but this is no longer the case, at least in our experience. And, while we don't long for the old disputes over "open" and "closed" membership, at least those conflicts meant that baptism was taken seriously.

Why such diminished interest? For some, believers' baptism, historically associated with exclusivism, has come to be seen as an ecumenical embarrassment—a reminder of division rather than a sign of unity. For others, however, Disciples practice is no longer distinctive enough. If we are going to be open to the sprinkling of infants, why make a big deal out of our different approach?

In this chapter, we want to insist that baptism should still be at the heart of who we are as Disciples of Christ. Ecumenical commitment, as we see it, does not mean filing down our distinctives. It means sharing our gifts for the sake of mutual enrichment in Christ's one body. The Disciples understanding of baptism is one of our tradition's greatest gifts.

Baptism and Disciples History

In the case of baptism, the basic Disciples text is not the *Declaration and Address*. The Campbells, like Barton Stone, were baptized as infants and only later became convinced that the immersion of believers, persons who can make their own decision of faith, is the baptism mandated by scripture and most appropriate to its biblical meaning.

The key figure in this shift was Alexander Campbell. Much has been written about Campbell's study of baptism after the birth of his daughter, and his subsequent conviction that whoever "has not been immersed in water…has never received Christian baptism"—a position at odds with that of Stone, who did not deny membership to the unimmersed, and Thomas Campbell, who thought his son's views on this matter would "paganize the church" by excluding unimmersed saints and martyrs.[3]

We want to concentrate, however, on Campbell's understanding of what baptism *means*. Campbell did not call baptism a "sacrament," preferring the term "ordinance"; however, he did hold that baptism, when coupled with repentance and faith, is the means through which God acts for the remission (forgiveness) of sins. The efficacy of baptism depends entirely on God's grace (which is why Campbell had to admit that persons sprinkled in infancy could be saved). Baptism is not a "work" we must perform. But *God's* work in baptism must be received in faith, and faith demands personal decision. No one can say "yes" to Christ on another's behalf.[4]

Baptism for the Remission of Sins

Three additional, and interrelated, points will help clarify this basic understanding. First, as we have noted, Campbell summarized the meaning of baptism by saying that it is "for the remission of sins" (sins actually committed, not guilt inherited from Adam). In baptism, penitent believers receive God's assurance of acceptance and pardon—which is the foundation of holy living. He puts it this way in *The Christian System:*

> Because forgiven, they [Christians] should forgive; because justified, they should live righteously; because sanctified, they should live holy and unblamably; because reconciled to God, they should cultivate peace with all [people], and act benevolently towards all; because adopted, they should walk in the dignity and purity of [children] of God; because saved, they should abound in thanksgivings, praises, and rejoicings, living soberly, righteously, and godly, looking forward to the blessed hope.[5]

We know full well, of course, that baptism as such guarantees nothing; there are plenty of baptized tyrants and unbaptized saints. If we grasp the import of God's grace, if we acknowledge our sin and trust in God's Word of pardon, then it is possible to live no longer for ourselves but for Christ and to give thanks that even this is a gift of the Spirit.

Baptism and Freedom

Second, believers' baptism recognizes and upholds people's freedom to affirm faith in Jesus Christ for themselves. It also recognizes and supports the church's freedom from interference by the state. An "established" church, in which baptism is practiced "indiscriminately," means that "the discrimination between the world and the church" is lost, the church's identity and witness severely compromised. Baptism, wrote Campbell, is the "Jordon flood" that, in some fundamental way, separates every Christian from the values of the nation or culture in which he or she happens to live.[6] The church shouldn't be a community of the lukewarm, of those who are Christian because their parents are or because it is socially expected. The church is a "peculiar people" who respond to God's grace by living as disciples of Christ, not of Caesar. Unlike the Anabaptists, however, this did not lead our movement to withdraw from society:

> For Campbell, baptism was for penitent believers ready to subject themselves to the command of the gospel to love God and neighbor. Such a view, he believed, had profound social implications, and he committed his movement to a transformation of society that he understood the gospel to command.[7]

Of course, believers' baptism guarantees nothing. In early twenty-first–century North America, churches practicing believers' baptism are often the ones most closely aligned with the economic and political establishment. Still, the baptism of those who make their own confession of faith can potentially mark a radical break in the person's life and, in turn, a radical distinction between the church and the society around it.

Baptism and the Family of Faith

Third, baptism is a sign that the person is adopted by God and received into a new family of faith. For Campbell, this is not a mere ceremonial entry into the church and is certainly not linked to membership in a local congregation. Baptism is a public declaration both of God's forgiveness and of one's incorporation into the church of all times and places. In the words of the Preamble to the Disciples *Design,* "Through baptism into Christ, we enter into newness of life and are made one with the whole people of God."[8]

As we have noted, many persons, whether baptized as infants or believers, live provincially, without regard for Christians in other places and other denominations. If we open ourselves to God's transforming grace, we can recognize through the sign of baptism that we now belong to Christ and, therefore, to all those others who also belong to him.

Baptism and Contemporary Implications

What are the implications for us today? To answer this question, let's approach this heritage from a slightly different angle. Churches such as ours that practice believers' baptism almost always begin with the conviction that the contemporary church, like the church of the early centuries, is in a missionary situation. At the risk of overgeneralizing, in the formative years of the church, ministry was leadership in mission; and baptism, though a means of grace, was a sign of commitment to that mission. Once Constantine made Christianity the established religion of the empire, however, ministry was frequently reduced to pastoral care, and baptism to a rite of passage. Alexander Campbell and colleagues thought they were restoring the pre-Constantinian church, a church of committed disciples who spread the good news of God's amazing grace in the midst of an antagonistic world.

The great mistake such churches usually make is to assume that a particular form of baptism leads to such discipleship. Experience tells us that people baptized as believers can be just as indifferent to God, just as allergic to mission, just as "immersed" in the surrounding culture as any other Christians. Meanwhile, millions of committed disciples were sprinkled as infants. The great strength of a tradition such as ours, however, is to insist that the church is in a missionary situation, that we do live in a culture that is antagonistic to the gospel. The way one is baptized guarantees nothing but believers' baptism, by emphasizing both God's gift of grace and our human response, underscores the fact that baptism has profound ethical and missional implications.

Baptism and Its Missional Implications

The first missional implication in baptism is that God's grace compels us to oppose discrimination based on such things as race, gender, and economic status. The most familiar baptismal formula in the New Testament is that found in Galatians 3: "As many of you as were baptized into Christ have clothed yourselves with Christ. There is no longer Jew or Greek, there is no longer slave or free, there is no longer male and female; for all of you are one in Christ Jesus" (vv. 27–28). These three identity markers—being a Jew, free born, and male—were what gave Paul his status in his own eyes and in the eyes of the world—until his encounter with the Risen Christ. Through baptism into him, all of these worldly status symbols were relativized; indeed, Paul now realized, they count for nothing since the one baptized is defined simply as Christian, as one who is in Christ.

What a difference this ought to make in the way we live. We (the authors of this book) are not Christian men, we are male Christians. Our identity comes as Christians, not as members of a particular gender. This new identity marker means that abuse directed at any female Christian is directed at us. We are not Christian Caucasians, we are Caucasian Christians. Our identity comes from Christ not from our race. This new identity means that discrimination aimed at African American sisters or brothers in Christ is aimed at us. It is one thing to say you will act against sexism or racism; it is another to realize that identity as a member or a race or gender is a matter of who you are.

The Galatians text is obviously talking about the identity of Christians and the inclusive nature of the church, but surely we are justified in seeing ethical as well as ecclesiological implications. The way we live as church, recognizing an essential oneness with people who are "different," is to be a model for the way people treat each other in society—starting with us. Racism, sexism, and classism in church and society are abominations to God that we oppose, not because we are good people, but because our very identity is at stake. That's what it means to be baptized.

Baptism and Universal Christian Solidarity

A second missional implication in baptism is that God's grace binds us in solidarity with Christians who suffer or celebrate anywhere in the world. The key biblical passage here is Paul's analogy of the body in 1 Corinthians 12: "For in the one Spirit, we were all baptized into one body..." (v. 13a). One member cannot say to another, "I have no need of you" (v. 21), or, "I don't belong to you." To the contrary, "If one member suffers, all suffer together with it; if one member is honored, all rejoice together with it" (v. 26). It is the apostle's greatest meditation on diversity and interdependence. The parts of the church are not the same; some may even be regarded as "weaker" or "less respectable." Yet, because of baptism, they are called to have "the same care for one another."

Let's make it all more concrete. The burden of foreign debt felt by brothers and sisters in the Congo is our burden. When a typhoon hits the Philippines, it is our tragedy (just as Katrina happened to them). AIDS in South Africa means, as one friend puts it, "that Christ's whole body is HIV positive." Of course, as human beings, we ought to be concerned with these things whether the victims are Christian, Muslim, or Rastafarian. There is, however, an even deeper claim on us as parts of the one church. That's what it means to be baptized.

Baptism and Rejection of Idolatry

A third missional implication in baptism is that God's grace calls and enables us to reject the idolatry—the love of money, the veneration of power—that is so much a part of our life in twenty-first–century North America. The great mission leader, Lesslie Newbigin, once contended that if the church in contemporary Europe and the United States were transported back to first-century Rome, the empire wouldn't even bother to persecute it![9] The empire could live with cults aimed at promoting the personal blessedness of their members in another world. What it couldn't abide was a "peculiar people" whose allegiance, indicated through baptism, was to God and God's kingdom—not Rome, Wall Street, or Washington, D.C.

Another of Paul's famous reflections on baptism is found in Romans 6: "Do you not know that all of us who have been baptized into Christ Jesus were baptized into his death? Therefore we have been buried with him by baptism into death, so that, just as Christ was raised from the dead by the glory of the Father, so we too might walk in newness of life" (vv. 3–4). Do we not know that our lives have been transformed?! We don't yet share in the full power of Christ's resurrection, but baptism is the sign that the enslaving power of sin has been broken. We are free from the need to draw identity or worth from transient things, free to live no longer for ourselves alone. Disciples biblical scholar Leander Keck puts it this way: "For Paul, baptism does not end mortality; it begins a new morality."[10] Our lives from this point on are defined by Christ, not idols of our own making. That's what it means to be baptized.

How might the Disciples practice of baptism be reformed to better reflect this understanding? We recommend the following ideas for serious consideration in congregations across the church.

Pre-baptism Instruction

One is rigorous instruction prior to baptism. Yes, God is the chief Actor in the sacrament, but one prepares for this defining moment by learning the story of our faith and learning from mentors about the ethical expectations that are part of one's response to the gospel. In this regard Protestants can take much from the "Roman Catholic Rite of Initiation for Adults" and learn from Jews and their preparation for Bar/Bat Mitzvah. In both instances candidates first learn the significance of the ritual through rigorous study before entering into it.

Disciples have sometimes been long on the act of baptism, but short on the necessary preparation for it. We spend weeks doing instruction on which other faiths and other Christian denominations spend months. The length of instruction does not equate to the quality candidates are receiving, but it does seem to us that Disciples could rethink the extent to which we undermine the importance we place on baptism by inadequate instruction for it.

Use of Strong Missional Language

A second recommendation is the use of strong missional language in the service of baptism. A good example, in our judgment, is found in the United Church of Christ's *Book of Worship* where the baptismal candidate is asked:

> Do you promise, by the grace of God, to be Christ's disciple to follow in the way of our Savior, to resist oppression and evil, to show love and justice, and to witness to the work and word of Jesus Christ as best you are able?

> Do you promise, according to the grace given you, to grow in the Christian faith and to be a faithful member of the Church of Jesus Christ, celebrating Christ's presence and furthering Christ's mission in all the World?[11]

We know of one Disciples pastor who asks newly baptized persons to name the ministry to which they feel called as part of the service. This, of course, presupposes instruction in the meaning of and opportunities for lay ministry that has been core to who Disciples are since the beginning of our movement.

Plan for Ecumenical Participation

A third recommendation is to plan for ecumenical participation in services of baptism. A person is not baptized into the Christian Church (Disciples of Christ) but into Christ's universal body. There is no better way to signify this theological claim than by including representatives of neighboring congregations in each baptism we perform. It is a visible reminder of our unity, the foundation of which is our common baptism.

Services of Renewing Baptismal Vows

Fourth, we recommend a service of renewal of baptismal vows in congregational and ecumenical settings. Such services can be found online. An example of renewing our baptismal vows as part of an Easter vigil is included in *Baptism and Belonging*, a worship resource for Disciples of Christ.[12]

A Final Word on Baptism and Identity

We end this chapter by returning to the basic theme of identity. In 1983, one of the authors of this book visited the Faroe Islands, a chain of eighteen islands, belonging to Denmark, in the middle of the North Atlantic. At the time of the visit (which was on behalf of the World Council of Churches), 80 percent of the Faroese belonged to the Danish Lutheran Church. In Denmark itself, nearly 90 percent of the population are baptized members of the "folk" (national) church, although only a small percentage worship regularly. In previous generations, almost everyone on the Faroes was Lutheran; but in recent decades, the Plymouth Brethren, a fundamentalist group of believers' Baptists, had grown by leaps and bounds.

The Plymouth Brethren refused to participate in meetings to welcome the WCC visitors, denouncing the whole idea of ecumenism in the local newspaper. One of us, however, did manage to meet with leaders of the community and to ask them, "What is your major complaint about the Lutheran folk church?" That unleashed a torrent! "They baptize everybody, so it doesn't mean a thing! A person shouldn't enter the church because it is part of their national identity. You become a Christian through repentance, change of heart. It involves a commitment, a decision, to live a new way. They act as if discipleship doesn't matter. Just baptize babies so you can count them, and then let them live like everybody else!"

Such language must sound familiar to anyone steeped in our own history. Believers' baptism traditions, at their best, preach a costly faith that calls for genuine commitment as those who follow the way of the Cross. But, the great problem with these traditions is that they tend, like the Plymouth Brethren, to be exclusivist, close-minded, anti-ecumenical—as if God were theirs, rather than the other way around. That's why we love being Disciples. At our best, we Disciples have been a most unusual combination of radical discipleship and ecumenical openness. We have practiced believers' baptism while seeking unity with those who practice differently. We have preached a costly faith without claiming that we have the last word on it—Christians only, but not the only Christians.

At the beginning of this chapter, we noted the emerging ecumenical consensus with regard to baptism. What we didn't note, however, is that the great majority of churches participating in that ecumenical work baptize infants. Overseas, only one believers' baptism tradition has become part of church unions in such places as North India, the United Kingdom, and Jamaica—the Disciples of Christ. In this country, eleven churches participate to some extent in Churches Uniting in Christ, only one of which baptizes believers as its normative practice—the Disciples of Christ.

We think a phrase that captures who we are is "bold humility"—bold in our proclamation and service, humble in our hospitality to those who are different. Baptism is a visible embodiment of this tension. Through baptism, God lays claim to us and turns us from other gods; but also through baptism, God unites us with the whole Christian family and opens us to persons unlike ourselves and perspectives unlike our own. Discipleship and openness. Bold mission and ecumenical humility. We believe that this is who we are as Disciples, and that it's an identity worth celebrating!

CHAPTER 6

Unity

One Church and One World

Peter Ainslie, a leading Disciples pastor in the early years of the twentieth century, declared in 1913 that the Disciples of Christ are "the first definitely organized movement in the history of the church for the healing of its schisms."[1] Scholars can debate whether Ainslie is historically correct, but he is surely on target with regard to Disciples self-understanding. Disciples historian Howard Short entitled one of his books from the 1950s *Christian Unity Is Our Business.* In the early years after Restructure, Disciples educator and mission leader, T. J. Liggett, assured fellow Disciples that the wholeness of the body of Christ remains "the dominant concept of our church."[2]

Once again, the *Declaration and Address* provides the foundational conviction: "The Church of Christ upon earth is essentially, intentionally, and constitutionally one; consisting of all those in every place that profess their faith in Christ and obedience to him in all things according to the Scriptures."[3] Unity, that is to say, is not a human creation but a gift of

God—an essential characteristic of the church. When Disciples gathered in 1909 to celebrate the centennial of the *Declaration and Address*, they listed "the unity...which Christ prayed might continue to exist among all those who should believe on Him"[4] as the number one principle for which the movement stands.

It seems to the authors of this book, however, that commitment to this "special calling" is waning among contemporary Disciples. Many active church members are unaware of this ecumenical legacy, in part because people today join congregations for reasons other than confessional heritage, and in part because little attention is paid, at least in our experience, to teaching about Disciples identity. Whatever the reason, we now have the appearance of being yet another denomination intent on self-perpetuation. "Take Christian unity out of the message of the Disciples," Ainslie once wrote, "and their existence only adds to the enormity of the sin of division by making another division."[5] This idea, repeated numerous times over the past two centuries, would come as a real surprise to many people in the pews of our contemporary congregations.

Even Disciples who support the ecumenical work of the church, however, may misunderstand important dimensions of this identity. Others see Christian unity as less important than work for evangelism (on the one hand) or peace and justice (on the other)—as if the proclamation of Christ, service in his name, and the wholeness of his body don't belong together in a proper understanding of church!

The purpose of this chapter is to restate this special calling to promote Christian unity in a way that, we hope, will engender new (or renewed) interest and commitment. More specifically, we will suggest that Disciples can appropriately be called "a movement for wholeness in a fragmented world"[6] in that, at our best, we have held together a passion for unity in the church with a passion for peacemaking in society. Despite the outstanding work done by Disciples historians, this is an underappreciated dimension of our identity—one that, we believe, holds real potential for helping to reinvigorate our ecumenical practice.

Different Meanings of Church Unity

We start with an understatement: Christian unity has meant different things to different people—and different churches. The Disciples, true to our heritage, have no definitive statement on what unity entails; but, beginning with the *Declaration and Address,* a broad understanding has emerged, shaped by interaction with other primary Disciples commitments. Ainslie argues, for example, that the Roman Catholic Church has, at times, maintained unity at the sacrifice of freedom, while Protestants have, at times, safeguarded freedom at the cost of unity.[7] Disciples have been unusual in insisting that Christians can express their oneness in Christ without a magisterium, standardized forms of worship, or hierarchical decision-making structures (although we have yet to prove that it can be so!).

The Urgency of Unity

Beyond the linking of unity and freedom, leaders in our tradition have often made the following claims. The first is that *unity is urgent.* Every student of Disciples history must surely be struck by the fervor with which the leaders of our movement have worked to undermine sectarian complacency in the body of Christ. The unity of Christians is not simply one item on a list of ecclesiastical priorities; it is the heart of the gospel, to be pursued and proclaimed with passionate urgency. Barton Stone: "If we oppose the union of believers, we oppose directly the will of God, the prayer of Jesus, the spirit of piety, and the salvation of the world."[8] Thomas Campbell: Division among Christ's followers is "anti-Christian," "antiscriptural," and "antinatural." It has "rent and ruined the Church of God." "In a word, it is productive of confusion and every evil work."[9] Peter Ainslie: "The greatest necessity of modern times is the unity of the Church of Christ. No other issue exceeds it in importance."[10]

As a result, Disciples historically have not seen our movement as a permanent part of the ecclesial landscape. Rather, in the words of a prominent Disciples pastor from the mid-twentieth century, we are "a denomination that hopes to die."[11] As late as the mid-1970s, Ronald Osborn could still long for the day "when Disciples no longer continue as a separate people but, finding a larger freedom in a united church, may share with others their experiment in liberty."[12] In our judgment, this passion for unity, this sense of distinctive mandate, this readiness to die for the sake of our calling, has given vigor to our evangelism, an edge to our social witness, and particular content to our worship and preaching. But is this still the case? If we have lost this urgency, is it any wonder that we seem to be adrift?

Unity as a Gift

A second claim is that *unity is given*. The foundation of the modern ecumenical movement is the biblically grounded conviction that there is one church thanks to the reconciliation that God has effected in Jesus Christ (e.g., 2 Cor. 5:16–20, Eph. 4:1–6). The ecumenical task, therefore, is not to create unity, but to address divisions of human making so the unity God has given may be visible to the world. Obviously, we have no shortage of divisions to address. We would be wrong to minimize their severity or significance. But the calling is "to become what we are"—a single body with many members, a single house with many stones, a single vine with many branches.

One implication of this insight is that unity is not synonymous with, or dependent on, human agreement. To claim that unity is constituted by our agreement on doctrine or social justice or anything else is a form of works righteousness. Of course, our theological differences must be reconciled if we are to confess Jesus Christ together before the world; but the argument made by such varied ecumenical leaders as William Temple, D. T. Niles, Suzanne de Dietrich, Willem Visser't Hooft, Albert Outler, and John Howard Yoder is that the hard work of reaching theological consensus is a *consequence* of our fundamental communion with Christ, not a prerequisite for it. The first assembly of the World Council of Churches put it succinctly: "Christ has made us his own and he is not divided."[13]

What we want to observe is that this same conviction that unity is primarily a divine gift and only secondarily a human achievement was present from the beginning of the Disciples movement and has appeared in key documents throughout our history. The most obvious expression is the famous proposition from the *Declaration and Address* quoted above: "The Church of Christ upon earth is essentially, intentionally, and constitutionally one." For the Campbells, a fragmented church is really no church at all.

Disciples historian Mark Toulouse underscores this point, noting that Stone's "Christians" and Campbell's "Disciples" would never have united in 1832 if the leaders had demanded full agreement from one another. What they did share was a conviction that "the unity of the church did not arise out of human origins, but rather must be experienced as the gift of God." Later in the century, writes Toulouse, Disciples thinking about unity began to change under the impact of such things as higher biblical criticism; but the notion that Christian oneness "simply is" remained constant.[14]

"Unity as given" was also the theme in several essays the Panel of Scholars wrote as the theological basis for Restructure. To take only one example, Ralph Wilburn observes, "If the unity of the church were merely something which religious men [and women] meet and decide upon, we would be at liberty to choose what class or race or cultural group should be included, and what excluded. But church unity is not so determined. The church is the body of Christ; it is a gift 'come down from above.'"[15]

Precisely this nature as gift from above gives the ecumenical movement its prophetic edge. Persons of different races, classes, nations, and political affiliations find themselves bound in fellowship, not because they agree on all things, but because through their communion with Christ they have communion with one another. No matter how estranged they are humanly speaking, in the body of Christ they cannot say, "I have no need of you." Their relationship is not an option; it is a gift.[16]

This understanding of unity as gift, however, is falling out of favor—especially in North American culture. The individualism of U.S. society, writes sociologist Robert Bellah, "finds it hard to comprehend...the idea that the church is prior to individuals and not just the product of them."[17] Our culture thinks of church as a voluntary association of like-minded folks who can shape the church however they please and who need not acknowledge uncomfortable relationships. Christians in Cuba... How can "they" be part of "us"? People in Disciple Heritage Fellowship (a conservative evangelical group) or, conversely, people in GLAD (a caucus for gay and lesbian Disciples and their supporters)... Let them leave the community! How can "we" have anything to do with "them"? But isn't the conviction that unity is a gift of God, not something dependent on our agreement, central to who we are as Disciples? If we have lost this conviction, is it any wonder that the power of our ecumenical witness is diminished?

Unity as Visible

The third claim is that *unity is visible*. Most Christians recognize that the unity of Christ's followers is a dominant scriptural theme, but many contend that such unity is a spiritual reality that need not (and, perhaps, cannot) be expressed through visible structures or other forms of overt fellowship. By way of contrast, the modern ecumenical movement has insisted that unity must be tangible enough that it makes a witness to the world of God's power to reconcile. The first purpose of the World Council of Churches, for example, is "to call the churches to the goal of visible unity in one faith and one Eucharistic fellowship expressed in worship and common life in Christ"[18]

Disciples have agreed. William Robinson, the outstanding British Disciples theologian, notes that our movement, unlike many Free Church Protestant groups, has "always denied the doctrine of the invisible church."[19] We have favored models of organic union, in which unity is clearly lived out through a common structure and identity, rather than loose federations of churches. As a result, Disciples have become part of organically united churches in such places as Jamaica, Great Britain, and North India, and have given major leadership to the U.S.-based Consultation on Church Union (now Churches Uniting in Christ). Is this still the case? Are we still champions of a substantive, visible oneness? If not, is it any wonder that our ecumenical identity has waned?

Unity as the Work of the Whole Church

Fourth is the claim that *unity is the work of the whole church.* It is often overlooked that the ecumenical movement was, at least in its early decades, a largely lay-driven effort to reform the church. Bishops and professional theologians certainly gave crucial leadership, but ecumenism's lifeblood flowed from the mission fields, the Sunday school movement, the YMCA and YWCA, Bible societies, and the Student Christian Movement—all of which were marked by lay leadership and constituency. In the nineteenth century, these efforts were generally distinct from the churches. One way of demarcating the start of modern ecumenism is when these lay movements and groups became concerned not just with the extension of evangelism and biblical literacy but with the renewal of these things within the life of the church itself. Over the past seventy-five years, however, the ecumenical movement has been gradually "professionalized," with ordained ecumenists assuming roles once filled by laypersons. All of this needs to be said carefully, especially with regard to our own church. The authors of this book give thanks to God for the work of the Disciples Council on Christian Unity. The occupants of that office have given, and continue to give, indispensable leadership. Clearly more needs to be done to teach the ecumenical vision of a church united and renewed in our congregations, to recover the lay character of our commitment to oneness in Christ. Disciples, of all Christians, cannot treat ecumenism as something best left to denominational specialists and theological experts. It is our identity as a people, not something done for us by an office in Indianapolis! If unity is not seen as the work of the whole church, is it any wonder that this part of our identity seems increasingly esoteric and irrelevant to many members?

Unity as a Symbol for One Humanity

This brings us to a theme running throughout the ecumenical movement that we suspect most Disciples leaders endorse, at least in theory. The unity of the church is inseparable from, and indispensable to, the wholeness of human society. The church, as a sign and anticipation of what God intends for all creation, doesn't just campaign for peace and justice; it must demonstrate *shalom* in the way its members live with one another if its witness is to be credible and compelling. If unity is simply a matter of structural merger, then it can be subordinated to such tasks as peacemaking and poverty relief. If, however, unity is understood as participation in God's work of reconciliation, then it is inseparably linked with the church's mission. Disciples, as we will suggest below, have not always held this tension adequately. The potential remains for us to make a highly unusual—and highly significant—witness.

In researching this chapter, we have been struck by the fact that many, if not most, of the leading unity advocates in our history have also been pacifists—that is, persons who were also deeply committed to peacemaking in human society. Alexander Campbell, for example, argued in his famous "Address on War" that "the precepts of Christianity positively inhibit war... The beatitudes of Christ are not pronounced on patriots, heroes, and conquerors, but on 'peacemakers' on whom is conferred the highest rank and title in the universe: 'Blessed are the peacemakers, for they shall be called the [children] of God.'"[20] In the first issue of the *Christian Baptist*, he wrote scathingly of those who pray for military victory through which are created the orphans and widows on which they can exercise their Christian charity. Later in life, he declared that Christian people can in no way countenance war as a means of redressing wrongs or settling controversies between nations. Among other things, it fragments the church and disgraces its Lord.[21]

Campbell was certainly not alone. Nearly every major figure of the movement in its first generations—including Thomas Campbell, Barton Stone, Raccoon John Smith, Robert Richardson, Moses Lard, Benjamin Franklin, Alexander Proctor, David Lipscomb, and J. W. McGarvey—were not only promoters of Christian unity but were committed to nonviolence.[22] "A nation professing Christianity, yet teaching, learning, and practicing the arts of war cannot be the kingdom of Christ," wrote Stone, "Nothing appears so repugnant to the kingdom of heaven as war."[23]

We have already noted that Peter Ainslie was the crucial figure in the early twentieth-century effort to reassert the centrality of unity for Disciples identity. He founded the Disciples Council on Christian Unity and championed our ecumenical vocation in such books as the wonderfully titled, *If Not a United Church —What?* But Ainslie was also a leading voice for peace at the onset of World War I, arguing that war is the greatest of all heresies: "Hardly anything could be more extremely opposite of Christianity than war."[24] Ainslie refused to concede that war could ever play a role in the quest for justice, because, as he saw it, the resort to arms renders any cause unjust.

In making such a witness for unity *and* peace, Ainslie was by no means on the fringe of our movement. For example, Charles Clayton Morrison, long-time editor of *The Christian Century*, was one of the foremost Disciples ecumenists in the first half of the twentieth century. His final book, *The Unfinished Reformation,* contended that denominational division is "a decadent survival of an era that is now past," and interpreted the ecumenical movement as a completion of the Protestant Reformation begun by Luther and colleagues four hundred years earlier.[25] Perhaps less well-known among Disciples, however, is Morrison's advocacy for peace in the aftermath of World War I. One of his books from the 1920s was entitled *The Outlawry of War,* in which he called for the churches, acting together, to promote an international declaration outlawing war and to insist on the creation of a world court to hold nations accountable for the violence they inflict. "How," he asked, "can we of the 'Christian' West have the face to preach brotherhood and peace and justice to the East when murderous war is still the ultimate judge in our civilization?"[26]

Morrison modified his pacifism and the editorial stance of *The Christian Century* after the U.S. was attacked by Japan in 1941, giving cautious support to American entry in World War II. This decision greatly disappointed his *Christian Century* colleague, and fellow Disciple, Harold Fey. Fey, who edited the second volume of *The History of the Ecumenical Movement* (a sign of his commitment to unity), also served as general secretary of the Fellowship of Reconciliation, the world's largest pacifist organization.

We have already made reference to the British Disciple, William Robinson, who contended that promotion of Christian unity is the only justification for our separate existence. Robinson, however, was also an ardent pacifist who maintained, to quote the title of one of his books, that *Christianity Is Pacifism.*

> Jesus gives us no laws to deal with war, slavery, money-making, or anything else. He does something better. He gives us the spirit of pacifism, of disinterested self-giving—a spirit which we are to work out in all personal relationships, both individual and social, no matter

what the cost and sacrifice to ourselves may be. And it is this spirit which when properly understood makes war positively irrational, devilish, and unthinkable. Christianity is pacifism.[27]

These same twin commitments can be found in many more recent leaders of our church—including T. J. Liggett, who once told us that he would go anywhere to speak on two themes: the unity of the church and the peace of the world. Even a brief review of our history shows that this is a very Disciples thing to say!

Of course, the real question is *why* any of this matters. The conjunction of unity and peace may seem, to many readers, self-evident. Divisions in the body of Christ often exacerbate political conflicts and hinder effective peacemaking. More theologically, God's gift of reconciliation is for *the world*; however, *the church*, in the words of the apostle Paul, is entrusted with this message of reconciliation—and it delivers this message not just by what it says or even by what it does, but by what it is. The church isn't just the bearer of the message of reconciliation; it is called and empowered to be the message embodied.

Unfortunately, however, Christians often separate what ought to be joined. In the history of the church, those who have emphasized peacemaking have often feared that unity would weaken the radical edge of their proclamation, while those who have emphasized unity have often feared that peacemaking would prove divisive. That is why the historic peace churches—Mennonites, Brethren, Quakers—have generally been sectarian, somewhat marginal to ecumenical life, while churches more inclined toward ecumenical engagement have generally affirmed a just war theology and left the question of whether or not to support a particular war to the individual conscience.

Since its first great conferences in the 1920s, the ecumenical movement has lived with this tension, trying to preserve global Christian fellowship in the face of World War II and the Cold

War. In one of the best books ever written on ecumenism, *And Yet It Moves,* Ernst Lange asserts, "The ecumenical movement is a movement for peace...is in fact the way in which the Christian churches really serve the cause of peace."[28] Because unity is a gift, "the church must manifestly be the church, still united as the one body of Christ, though the nations wherein it is planted fight each other."[29]

Again, however, actual practice has often failed to match such rhetoric. The report from the WCC's Vancouver Assembly (1983) offers a realistic assessment:

> For some the search for a unity in one faith and one eucharistic fellowship seems, at best secondary, at worst irrelevant to the struggles for peace, justice, and human Dignity; for others, the church's involvement against the evils of history seems, at best secondary, at worst detrimental to its role as eucharistic community and witness to the gospel.[30]

This tendency to split the agenda has frequently been institutionalized in churches and ecumenical organizations. "Peace" and "unity" are relegated to separate departments, setting up a competition for resources and influence. Disciples have also been guilty of playing one off against the other—or, at least, of not bringing them together. Alexander Campbell was an outspoken pacifist—in times of peace. However, during the Mexican War of 1846, he refrained from calling for an end to the violence lest such a call prove divisive for Disciples fellowship.[31] To take a more recent example, at the General Assembly in 1985, Disciples voted both to enter an Ecumenical Partnership with the United Church of Christ, one of the most significant unity developments of recent decades, and to receive the most substantial report on peacemaking ever produced by our church, *Seeking God's Peace in a Nuclear Age.* Nothing at the Assembly, however, indicated that these two acts had anything to do with one another, that unity and peace might be part of a whole vision of church. The peace report itself observes that we "have scarcely begun to ask what the unity of the church means with regard to war."[32]

It is also true—and shocking!—that few of the Disciples authors mentioned above made explicit connection between church unity and peace; the tendency to compartmentalize infects us all. The one real exception is Ainslie, as the following passage makes clear:

> In the years to come the charge will be laid against the church of this day that because of its divisions, and therefore its unspiritual attitudes, the whole world is under the domination of social and economic wrongs, culminating in the disastrous war of 1914... At the crisis of 1914 organized Christianity stood helpless in every nation on the globe and was powerless to preserve the peace of the world. Surely division has its fruit. Whatever may be the immediate causes, the remote cause of [World War I] must be laid at the door of the church.[33]

War, as Ainslie saw it, is the ultimate church division, and church unity is the ultimate witness to peace. Both the church's endorsement of state violence and its acquiescence to fractures caused by culture, race, or ideology show just how far Christians have strayed from the vision of the New Testament. "When Christians no longer kill one another but willingly die for one another, all nations shall come to know the love of God, which can only be made known as the cross perpetually proclaims it."[34]

Of course, not all Christians will agree with a call to peace. Ainslie's opposition to the First World War did not enhance his popularity with many Disciples of his day! He was certainly aware that a commitment to unity entails a willingness to live with hawks as well as doves in the communion of the church. (After all, unity is not a product of human agreement!) But what impresses us is that Ainslie did not allow this conviction to temper his insistence that peace is at the heart of the gospel. We don't drum those who support war out of the church, Ainslie would say, but the burden of proof is on them to show how such support is consistent with scripture and not simply an attempt to enlist religion in a nationalist cause.

Speaking now for ourselves, we insist that at times Christians must say, "No, *that* is not the gospel," standing against the position of brothers and sisters in the church. Even in such moments, however, we also must affirm that the "them" we oppose are, in some fundamental sense, "us." An ecumenically oriented church cannot fear the controversy that comes with prophetic witness, for that is paralyzing; but it must, at all times, hate division because the story by which we live tells us that we have been linked in communion with persons we otherwise would shun. Can there be a more profound testimony to peace?

Can Disciples reclaim this extraordinary heritage? Can our own history help us to recognize that ecumenism, sometimes dismissed as irrelevant to the social struggles of the twenty-first century, is in fact desperately relevant in this age of seemingly perpetual violence? Can we demonstrate to church and society that it is possible to be both reconciling *and* prophetic?

The authors of this book believe we can, but it will take a conscious effort on the part of Disciples ministers at every level of the church to bring focus to this need. We hope we have made the case that unity is a critical element in who we are and how we live out the gospel as a community of faith. Jean Vanier, the founder of the L'Arche Communities for severely mentally and physically handicapped persons around the world, says true Christian community is a place where people are growing in love and peacemaking.[35] Love is, of course, the basis of unity—love that has the will to remain together when the pressures are to split apart. So love gives birth to unity, and unity is expressed in peacemaking. These are qualities of the

Christian gospel. Disciples came into existence because of the vision our founders had that the church of Christ on earth could embody unity and peacemaking. Because we have not yet realized this hope is no reason to abandon it. Neither is it cause for softening our commitment to the qualities of unity and peacemaking that give it substance. Rather, the challenge is to highlight them even more as a way to call the church to greater faithfulness to the gospel. We cannot be Disciples and not seek to heal the church of its divisions and, thus, model for the world a life together marked by peace and justice.

CHAPTER 7

Mission

The Ministry of Reconciliation

Every Christian denomination, organization, and movement in the nine century understood the Christian mission as "making disciples": "Go therefore and make disciples of all nations..." (Mt. 28:19). Their commitment to this mission led our founders to focus on the divisions denominationalism represented. They believed such divisions were a serious barrier to fulfilling the Great Commission. The unity of the church, therefore, and the attending rejection of the use of creeds as tests of faith, were born of a passion for evangelism. As Alexander Campbell wrote: "Our opposition to creeds arose from a conviction that, whether the opinion in them were true or false, they were hostile to the union, peace, harmony, purity, and joy of Christians, and adverse to the conversion of the world to Jesus Christ."[1]

Disciples and the Great Commission

While Disciples today continue to speak about the Great Commission, it is not with one voice as it once was. Some among us believe the traditional understanding of the Matthew

81

text noted above stems from a misleading translation, that a more accurate reading of the verse is, "Go, therefore, and *teach* all nations…" The word translated "teach" is *matheteuo*, which literally means "to disciple, to enroll as scholar, to instruct," suggesting that the English translation "make" creates the false impression that Christians can make "disciples" out of people when in fact that it is the work of the Holy Spirit. Moreover, the translation "make" tends to overshadow the fact that the best teacher is one who models what is being taught. Thus, the church is an effective teacher of the gospel only insofar as it models the gospel.

Others among us consider this kind of discussion an effort to justify the lack of passion for evangelism that has been a primary reason for our numerical decline. These contrasting views have been with Disciples for many years. As Mark Toulouse has noted, personal evangelism was the focus of Disciples foreign missions prior to 1928, but thereafter it began to evolve into relational mission characterized more by issues of justice than individual conversion[2] as we turned to indigenous Christians for mission leadership. It also may have been this tension that led to the Mission Imperative adopted by the General Board in 2000, which described the Disciples mission as "To be and to share the good news of Jesus Christ, witnessing, loving, serving from our doorstep to 'the ends of the earth' (Acts 1:8)."

To *share* the good news suggests personal evangelism. To *be* the good news suggests the role of teaching for the church. But more than this, it suggests the imperative of our unity emphasis. "Being" the good news underscored that the church is called to be a sign, that it witnesses by the way it lives, not just by what it says or does, but by who it is. Thus, the General Board was calling Disciples to the mission of evangelism while leaving its meaning open to interpretation. It also added to the statement a call for congregational life to be strengthened in order to fullfill this mission. But two major questions were left unanswered:

"What does it mean to be and share the good news?" and, "How do we build up congregations for this task?"

Soon after the General Board accepted the statement, two goals were set forth by then General Minister and President, Richard Hamm, as a practical way to live out the imperative. Whether or not these goals were intended to become a consuming focus of the statement is unclear, but that is what has happened. The first one was to start one thousand new congregations by the year 2020. The second goal was to revitalize an equal number of established congregations. To date we are more than half way toward a thousand new congregations. The progress on revitalization of existing churches has been less dramatic. Admittedly, though, measuring new life in old congregations is harder than counting new church starts.

Not everyone is applauding the pace of the first goal. Those who are supporting that pace seem to believe new congregations represent the hope for Disciples, especially with the influx of minorities this initiative has produced. Those who are not supportive worry that we are mistaking numbers for new life, especially when many of the new congregations are not "new," but simply new to Disciples, as regions grant recognition to heretofore non-Disciples churches without any sustained process for teaching them the particularities of our identity and practices. When this issue is raised, the charge of racism is often made, as if being concerned about identity and practice is a veil behind which intolerance and establishment power is at work.

These questions aside, the dual commitment to new church starts and transforming established congregations as a way to put the Mission Imperative into action underscores the fact that Disciples have always shown the dexterity of being able to do mission without having a definitive understanding of what it means to follow the Great Commission. This is not a bad thing, but it seems to these authors that as theological differences among Christians have become more pronounced, it will become increasingly more difficult to walk this tightrope, especially as Disciples try to understand the implications of being a church in a religiously plural world, a subject to which we will return at the end of the chapter. First, we want to posit a way forward that can help to unify Disciples around a common understanding of mission. Ironically, to do this we need to think, not about mission, but about identity.

The connection between identity and mission runs throughout the Bible. Being a covenant people determined what Israel did. The two primary questions the people asked were, "Who are we?" and "What are we to do?" The latter depended on the former, not the other way around.

Mission and Reconciliation

Apparently the apostle Paul had this relationship in mind when he explained the Christian mission to the Christians in Corinth:

> So if anyone is in Christ, there is a new creation: everything old has passed away; see, everything has become new! All this is from God, who reconciled us to himself through Christ, and has given us the ministry of reconciliation; that is, in Christ God was reconciling the world to himself, not counting their trespasses against them, and entrusting the message of reconciliation to us. So we are ambassadors for Christ, since God is making his appeal through us; we entreat you on behalf of Christ, be reconciled to God. For our sake he made him to be sin who knew no sin, so that in him we might become the righteousness of God. (2 Cor. 5:17–21)

Paul's life had been turned upside down by his encounter with Jesus on the Damascus Road, as if he had become a whole new person. He understood this kind of transformation as the work of God that could and should happen to anyone who comes to faith in Jesus. This experience of God's power working through faith was for Paul like being alienated from someone, and then being reconciled by that person's graciousness toward you as any wrongdoing is wiped away. The natural response to such grace is to act the same way toward others. As you have been reconciled to God, he says to the Corinthians, so be reconciled to one another.

But there is a catch. This ministry of reconciliation is not something they can do unless and until the reconciling work of God has gotten inside them. The word "entrust" doesn't imply this, which is why it is not a helpful translation. The original word *tithemi* is better translated "sink down" or "put inside." To be "entrusted" with the message of reconciliation suggests it is something we hold in our hands, something that is external. *Tithemi* points to just the opposite experience. The ministry or service of reconciliation arises from within. God, Paul says, has put reconciliation in us in order for it to come out of us in the form of service. God, then, makes an appeal for reconciliation to the world through the people in whom it resides. This is consistent with Paul's earlier assertion that anyone who is in Christ is a "new creation." With reconciliation being "sunk" deep down into their very being, how could it be otherwise?

This passage underscores the linking of mission and identity common to biblical material. The mission of the church is not something we do. It is something we are, which may account for Stanley Hauerwas and Will Willimon making the case that the most political thing the church can do is to be the church.[3] We don't engage in reconciliation ministry unless it is already in us to do so. If it isn't, we won't do it. If we try, it will be apparent that it is not authentic. Thus, the extent to which we become instruments of reconciliation depends on the width and breath of it being inside us. Even more, we read Paul as saying that the ministry of reconciliation isn't tangential to being ambassadors for Christ in the world. It is constitutive to it. In short, reconciliation is what Christians do as witnesses to

God's good news in Jesus Christ because reconciliation is who we are. Being in Christ has made us people of reconciliation, and being people of reconciliation is how we show the world we are in Christ.

This call of God to the ministry of reconciliation underscores the most significant shift in mission theology in the past half century, arising from within the ecumenical movement, the focus on "Missio Dei." Beginning as early as 1952, ecumenical leaders began emphasizing that it is God's mission in which the church participates. From this perspective the church does not have a mission. Rather, God's mission has a church. What this meant in practice was that evangelism began to be understood as one mission point among many. Calling people to Christ was not all that God is up to. Combating racism, working for peace, seeking justice in all its forms were also mission. The church was the community of Christ working on behalf of the mission of God.

This understanding of the interrelatedness between identity and mission was written into the former Division of Homeland Ministries principles and statement in 1981, setting a historical precedent for Disciples of linking mission with reconciliation, evangelism with justice seeking, witnessing with the social gospel. We believe this linkage remains a valid foundation for Disciples today building a consensus around evangelism. Words and actions are equally tools for fulfilling the Great Commission. The message we speak has to be put into action. The church must model its own words. Being reconcilers in the name of Jesus can be the identity Disciples project to the world. Thus, mission is not something we decide to do; mission is an essential expression of the people we are and are seeking to become. Mission and identity. Identity and mission. Two sides of the same coin. Two fruits from the same tree. Two parts of a whole life committed to putting God first. The word that makes the content of both specific is *reconciliation*.

As familiar as the mission of reconciliation sounds, it may be more radical than we suppose. Paul uses the word *katallasso* for "reconciliation." The root is *allasso* and means "to make different," "to exchange one thing for another thing." Paul believed God made the divine/human relationship different in Jesus Christ. Those who experience it through faith immediately begin to act in ways that make a difference in the world. They exchange an immoral lifestyle for a godly lifestyle. For Paul *reconciliation* summarized what that difference was. Reconciliation is not only what God has accomplished through Christ in the divine/human relationship, it is the goal toward which our relationship with one another is directed. The key, though, is understanding that Christians don't do reconciliation except as we are reconcilers. The old mental frame called us to be agents of reconciliation. The new image calls us to become reconcilers.

Throughout this book we have been discussing those aspects of our common life that seem to us to express who we are, and, therefore, what we are to be doing. We have tried to affirm our identity and to ground it in our heritage. We have also attempted to be provocative about our present practices, as well as being both honest and hopeful about our future. To further this focus on the relationship between identity and mission, we want to set forth in a systematic way some conclusions to which we think the previous chapters have led us as we think about mission. Further, because Disciples now work in other nations by developing and depending upon indigenous leadership, we believe these conclusions are also appropriate to our historic commitment to world mission, especially as we work in and through ecumenical partnerships. Indeed, Disciples have evolved in our understanding of mission to the point where the relationship between identity and mission that can guide adaptation to diverse cultural settings here at home can also be used in our work abroad.

Commitment to Covenant

Our first conclusion is that identity and mission cannot function in a community of faith that extols the virtue of diversity without having a genuine commitment to covenant. Without covenant, diversity becomes another word for unresolved divisions we don't want to admit exist between us. Neighborhoods, nations, and churches can be diverse and also anything but united. This turns diversity into divisions by another name. As we said earlier, covenant is a commitment Disciples made to one another in Restructure that, while more on paper than a lived reality, remains the visible expression of the mystery of belonging to one another because we belong to Christ. What we often forget is that a commitment to covenant even as we fail to live it holds the potential for transformation. A bad marriage always has a chance to become better as long as the two people are committed to making it work. Breaking covenant hurts community, but not taking it seriously destroys it.

Diversity means "differing from one another, a composition of unlike and distinct qualities."[4] This is a marvelous description of spiritual gifts in the church. But without covenant these differences evolve into conflicts that create sub-group rivalry. No institution has had more experience with this happening than the Protestant movement—including, of course, Disciples. We know this history and, yet, continue to repeat it. One obvious lesson in this respect is that Christians are no less prone to rejecting the necessity of compromise for the sake of covenant than secular groups. Compromise is what makes diversity work. Too many of us have the mistaken notion that compromise means giving up one's integrity.

In a telling scene in *To Kill a Mockingbird,* Atticus Finch asks his six-year-old daughter, Scout (Jean Louise) if she knows what a compromise is. She responds, "bending the law." That is what many adult Disciples (and disciples) would also say. Atticus responds to her, "No, it means an agreement reached by two parties through mutual consent." That agreement necessitates concessions by all involved. No concessions means no agreement. Agreement is what compromise produces, and compromise is how diversity functions in community. Only compromise makes blending differing qualities possible. Far too often, compromise is seen as a coward's way, while rigidity of viewpoint is hailed as virtuous. Of course, the opposite is the case. Compromise is virtuous because it is a sign that one admits to the possibility of being wrong. Rigidity is a vice because it is an expression of hubris.

Covenant makes diversity rich and powerful because it brings flexibility to the table. If we are to be a united church instead of simply talking about Christian unity, diversity within covenant must become a primary commitment. Without it, we will be guilty of talking a good game when it comes to reconciliation without actually being reconcilers within our own family of faith.

Mission and Institutional Amnesia

Our second conclusion says we believe Disciples will continue to live in fear of death as long as institutional amnesia remains prevalent. Americans in general have little knowledge of history. Christians are no exception, most especially when it comes to the church. Yet a knowledge of history is the antidote to forgetting who we are as a church, and, with it, what we are called to do. For this reason we suggest that the best thing we could do to generate a renewed passion for mission is to promote and institute a churchwide study of Disciples history. Losing a sense of purpose is common in groups unless they are intentional about educating new members in their history. Because so many Disciples think we have no defining story, we have trouble finding a consensus around a shared ethos. But we do have a story, and all of us should know it and be able to tell it well.

Scripture assures us that perfect love casts out fear. Love is amorphous until it is embodied in specific relationships. Once it grows beyond our immediate family, it becomes a communal experience. The more we know about that community, the closer we are bound to everyone in it. This is why knowing our story, our history, is important to living out of an abundance of love rather than being overcome by fear. We jokingly say to one another that Disciples are the best-kept secret in America, but it is no laughing matter. If it is true, it is not because we don't tell others about us. Rather, it is born of an institutional amnesia that leaves large numbers of us ignorant about what makes us who we are. If you don't know who you are, you have nothing to say to someone else about yourself.

Worse, perhaps, is that institutional amnesia greatly diminishes a collective sense of mission. As much as we want to believe mission itself is a sufficient motivation, experience suggests otherwise, partly because mission must have longevity to make a difference. To know you are doing what you are doing because not doing so would contradict who you are is the key to a sustained mission. Disciples share the good news in word and deed because that is who we always have been. The passion for the oneness of the church that gave birth to the Disciples movement grew from the spirit of reconciliation that already existed inside our founders. This is why they pursued the visible unity of the church against great odds. They gained sustenance from the two primary acts of the church—baptism and the Lord's Supper. We focused on each of them earlier for this reason. They not only reach back to New Testament Christianity, they remind us of our roots as a people called Christians and Disciples. In short, they connect us to Jesus and to our Disciples heritage. Thus, to know who our founders were is to know who we are, and, thus, what we are called to do.

We believe Disciples leaders need to give more attention to identity, if we hope to build a passion for mission. New churches do need to know the stream of tradition into which they are stepping, while transformation of established congregations must include a reaffirmation of their role in that tradition. We believe an identity crisis lurks beneath the surface of our life together, perhaps a long time in coming, but certainly exacerbated by numerical and financial decline. Few leaders have expressed concern or alarm about it. Instead, decline has been met with responses that have more to do with symptoms than causes. Parents tell their come-of-age children never to forget who they are, their roots. Roots are essential for identity. Teaching the Disciples story is a pressing need that cannot be left to seminaries and books. Both play an important role, but they cannot substitute for congregational pastors and regional ministers making this a priority. Commitment to mission is one of those aspects of ministry that is a by-product, not a goal. If we know our story as Disciples, we will become the mission we should be fulfilling.

What can facilitate this immersion in learning our story? The various Disciples expressions of church must conclude any historical review with a collective effort to write an identity statement. Until recently, this has not received much attention. The focus has, instead, been on mission statements, revealing a serious neglect of the relationships between identity and mission. A positive step is the identity statement from the Vision Team noted in chapter 1. We are also pleased that the General Board has given its support, indicating a growing awareness that practice cannot be understood apart from identity and that identity is revealed in practice.

Disciples and Religious Pluralism

This brings us back to the relationship between Disciples in mission and the reality of religious pluralism we mentioned earlier in the chapter. Today's America has a religious environment radically different from what our founders confronted, which carries profound implications for how we understand and fulfill the Great Commission. At one time here in our country, people who had a spiritual itch would look no further than the nearest church to have it scratched. That is no longer the case. More Islamic temples are being built across the United States than new churches. Christians might view this change with alarm and redouble their efforts to evangelize the nation. While all of us can affirm the efficacy of living the gospel in ways that attract non-Christians to want to know about Jesus, the question remains as to the appropriate attitude Christians should have toward people of other faith traditions.

It seems to us that the historic Disciples commitment to ecumenism has prepared us for such as time as this to show the way for other Christians to follow. In 1989 the World Conference on Mission and Evangelism of the World Council of Churches meeting in San Antonio approved a statement affirming that the church witnesses to the salvation it knows in Jesus Christ even as it does not put limits on God's grace. This is an affirmation we believe Disciples can also make. Building on our historic claim that we are Christians only, but not the only Christians, the 1989 Conference invites us to expand this statement to say that we are the people of God only, but not the only people of God. This would reflect the Disciples continuing efforts to build interfaith bridges of understanding and reconciliation.

The challenge arising from our commitment to the Christian mission in today's world is to have the courage and foresight to expand the Christian understanding of what it means to worship a sovereign God who is Creator of the whole earth and who dwells in it. The incendiary nature of religious conflict that is making Middle East peace efforts more difficult reminds us of the urgent need for a mission imperative involving reconciliation between the children of Abraham. Jews, Christians, and Muslims must learn to live together, or we will continue to die together. Can Disciples who have been at the forefront of intra-faith dialogue now take the lead in a worldwide expansion of inter-faith bridge building? Doing so will involve a new understanding of Christianity's role in a religious plural world. Are we ready to accept that the validity of Christianity does not depend upon the invalidity of other religious traditions? Are we willing to acknowledge that we can tell all the truth we know without claiming to know all the truth there is?

The Mission Imperative of 2000 declared that Disciples are to be and to share the good news of Jesus Christ. But historical realities always impact the church's mission. Our founders confronted a Christian community fractured and divided to the point of undermining any witness to reconciliation. We believe the whole of the Christian community faces a similar challenge in today's world of religious pluralism. Our willingness to expand our former statement of identity will reveal the degree to which we understand afresh that the ministry of reconciliation we are called to embody confronts new circumstances. We have the opportunity to declare without equivocation that we are a people who serve God only, and rejoice that others not of our household are willing to make the same claim.

CHAPTER 8

Congregation

Church but Not the Whole Church

"That institution which separates us from the world, and consociates the people of God into a peculiar community," wrote Alexander Campbell, "...is the congregation or church of the Lord." He went on to say, "The true Christian church, or house of God, is composed of all those in every place that do publicly acknowledge Jesus of Nazareth as the true Messiah, and the only Savior of men...and are walking in his ordinances and commandments—and of none else."[1] The church was not a single congregation, he was quick to add, but a "community of communities" that cooperates with one another in prayer, respect for one another, and in ministry.

Church as Community of Communities

This understanding of the church as a community of communities consciously or intuitively lay behind the vision twentieth-century Disciples had when they called for a restructuring of their life together into three areas— General, Regional, Congregational—each being a legitimate manifestation of the one Church of Christ on earth. Though Campbell specifically spoke only of "districts" existing beyond a single congregation, it was not a major leap for later Disciples to understand that all areas of our life together were rightful expressions of church. Looking back, it seems fair to say that theirs was a grand vision of church and an inevitable culmination of the evolution of a movement of people joined in discipleship and who together wanted to be the church in an effective and efficient way.

Unfortunately, the vision and the reality turned out to be something altogether different. The growth of staffs, units, and programming led to an expanding bureaucracy that soon began to see the church at the congregational level as a source of funding rather than as the foundation of the ministry of the whole church. As disagreements over Disciples policies, pronouncements, and overall direction grew, tension began to characterize the relationship between the three manifestations of the church. The heirs of Alexander Campbell had sought to embody his vision of cooperation between the various communities that composed the community called the church, but in the process had neglected his warning that the "manner of cooperation" is what ultimately mattered. A reckoning was bound to take place. Only for Disciples it was quite subtle. Financial support for the General and Regional manifestations of the church began to decline as congregations started speaking with their pocketbooks.

At its best the concept in the *Design* adopted in 1968 was intended to remind us as a people that there are things we can do together that we cannot do alone. It remains an important principle, but our numerical decline and financial instability as a denomination have revealed a disturbing weakened state of the majority of our congregations. Hidden in our desire to believe that each manifestation of the church—General, Regional, and Congregational—is an equal partner has been a reluctance to admit that the healthiness of the first two is dependent on the strength of the third. This is not to suggest that General and Regional problems do not affect congregations. They obviously do, but this does not translate into congregations being dependent on Regions or the General Church for their existence as is the case in reverse.

We recognize that decline in congregational spirit and ministry, size and commitment, has many causes. It is tempting when discussing congregational life among Disciples to oversimplify the issues and problems facing us. This often creates conflict between those who believe there are serious problems in our common life that must be addressed and those who believe critics are simply seeing the glass as half empty. We believe many good things can be said about Disciples life, but we also reject the notion that criticism is equivalent to pessimism. The critical comments we are making throughout this book arise from our desire to strengthen our common life as a church. Moreover, we believe that if the whole church has suffered because of the decline of our congregations, as we are suggesting, it is reasonable to think the whole church will benefit from a transformation of them. But transformation necessarily begins with an assessment of where we are at a given moment.

Our sense is that we do need to worry about some things as we think about Disciples congregations, such as the following: an aging membership, a growing dropout rate among seniors who no longer feel tied to their churches; the struggle to attract young families; the loss of energy and funding for the mission of the church in general and the work of reconciliation among the poor and dispossessed in particular; the erosion of denominational identity; and the decline of denominational loyalty. It is not an exaggeration to say that in large measure we Disciples are a shell of our old self. What is more, the reality is finally dawning on many congregations that past decline has become permanent. The pendulum swing they were sure would come back their way is not going to happen.

A Called People

But as much as none of us likes what has happened to us, we want to suggest that the current predicament presents us with some exciting challenges we are confident all levels of our church can meet. The church's future does not lie in its past. Rather, it depends on Christians of every generation being able to adapt to being the church in the circumstances they confront. Though our founders were far from perfect in understanding the Bible or the nature of the church and its ministry, they were nonetheless courageous and determined as they sought to strike out in a new direction from the denominationalism of their time that was dividing the church and weakening its witness in the world. Can we show the same courage and determination? We believe the answer is Yes.

If the church is the ecclesia, the "called out" in the name of Christ, the congregation is the "called together" of those who have already responded to the call to come out of the world into the body of Christ and now want to learn how to live that way. This seems to us to capture Campbell's view that a congregation is the tangible expression of those who are being shaped into a peculiar people. But what it means to live as this peculiar community has been a struggle in every generation since the first century. The paradox of Christian history is that while everything has changed since the time of Jesus, nothing has changed. Christians are still trying to learn how to live in the world, but not be of it.

Measuring Congregational Strength

We have seen enough throughout our history as Disciples to understand that numbers tell us very little about the strength of the church or of a congregation. Large and small churches can be faithful and unfaithful. There are numerous examples of congregations that have sacrificed faithfulness as they faced important issues such as racism, sexism, homosexuality, and many others in order to preserve their numbers. All of us want Disciples congregations to grow numerically, but what is more important is their spiritual health. Churches are not organizations. If we take Paul's metaphor of the church as the body of Christ seriously, it is natural to focus on spiritual healthiness as the biblical measure of a congregation's life. It can be big or small, short or tall, but none of that has anything to do with its state of health. Just as an individual can outwardly show signs of doing well but be inwardly unhealthy, so can congregations. They can look fine on the outside, but be inwardly suffering. They can even prosper financially and numerically, but still be spiritually dead.

Healthiness for a church has many manifestations, but all of them express something quite simple to understand—spiritual maturity. The question every church should ask itself is how spiritually mature it actually is. In making this assessment the first point of concern becomes obvious. In large measure church members have been schooled in the institutional needs of church membership without necessarily being equipped for discipleship. This is the dilemma institutionalism has created. So much of a congregation's time, talent, and resources are spent in maintenance ministry that enables congregations to do what they are doing without asking if this is what they should or could be doing as the body of Christ. Thus, to many church members the call to self-denial, to prophetic ministry, to waging peace rather than war, to unrelenting forgiveness often sounds like political partisanship rather than Christian discipleship. What this tells us is that it is easy enough to believe in Jesus. It takes some effort, but not a lot, to profess Jesus as Savior and Lord, be baptized, and become a member of the church. It is much more effort-full to make this decision a first step in a life-long journey of learning how to live the Christian life in the modern world, or as our founders put it, being a community of people who live under the Lordship of Christ.

Confronting the Reality of Change

Traveling the distance between who we are when we enter the church and what we begin to become as a follower of Jesus requires a commitment to change. Remaining the same is not an option for anyone serious about discipleship. But of course, change is work, hard work in fact. If it were easy, everyone would do it. All of us would do whatever it takes to be healthy, happy, and productive. We would adapt to changing circumstances without complaint. But we know none of that is true. Change is unsettling for all of us, which means that as urgent as congregational transformation is, in practice we resist it. This is ironic for Disciples, because we began as a change movement in American Christianity. Our history suggests that Disciples congregations ought to be models for change.

But this is hardly the case. It is not that we do not know change is inevitable in life. But as Alvin Toffler predicted in his 1970 book, *Future Shock*, the rapidity of change can be overwhelming to the human psyche. Indeed, he may have understated its impact. Change now happens at warp speed. Consider the fact that when Bill Clinton was elected president in 1992, virtually no one had e-mail, "E-Commerce" was a dream, and "blogging" wasn't even an idea. American jobs being outsourced to India and other places to the extent that developing nations have now become major players in the world of technology was once unimaginable. All of this has happened in a matter of a few years, and we are all struggling to regain our balance in a world where yesterday was a minute ago.

Fully Embracing Being Disciples

The fact that we know change is both inevitable and fast doesn't make it easier to adapt to new realities, but without this recognition, coping becomes more difficult. At the same time, the rapidity of change means no one can predict with certainty what will be required of us tomorrow. This is why spiritual maturity is so important. It is how we equip ourselves to confront what may happen. As Disciples preacher Fred Craddock is fond of saying, we may be born again, but we are not born full grown. No one jumps from infancy to full maturity. Growth can be slow, but it can also be steady, putting down roots that will produce good fruit.

This book is our statement that we believe the best days for Disciples are ahead of us. In the final chapter we will discuss the specifics of how this is the case for us as a denomination. Here our concern is the congregation, given the fact that it is the cornerstone for our collective life. What can Disciples congregations do to strengthen them for the future? Our answer may at once surprise and disappoint you, but we ask that you hear what we have to say before making final judgment. We believe the key to the life of Disciples congregations is to embrace the theme of this book—reclaiming our identity and reforming our practices. In this age some call postdenominational, we are convinced that because of the particularity of who we are as Disciples, by boldly embracing that identity our congregations will offer a viable alternative to the empty promises of the dominant American culture. In short, we are suggesting that the key to the future of Disciples congregations is to be thoroughly and wholly *Disciples*. What we want to do is to explain what this would look like. One of the things that will become clear as we proceed is that effective leadership is indispensable to strong congregations and certainly congregational transformation. Initially we considered combining the two into one chapter, finally choosing instead to give each of them separate treatment. But the overlap between the two will be apparent in both.

The Congregation as a Covenant Community

In the first chapter we sought to make the case that being a covenant community of faith is the sum of how Disciples live and work together. The fact that we have not lived by covenant as well as we could have is itself an invitation for congregations to do better. Covenant at the congregational level can serve as the foundation for it being done more effectively at the Regional and General Church levels. What is more, being covenant communities can speak to the times in which we live. People are hungry for genuine community, not least because it is a rare experience for them. The need to belong, to be welcomed into the lives of others as we are, is a basic need in today's world, where social, economic, racial, sexual, and political barriers separate us. Disciples congregations are made for such a time as this. Our heritage is one that insists that in Christ all human creed and actions are secondary to devotion to the oneness created by belonging to him. There is a reason Disciples have been at the forefront of church efforts to bring about social justice. As we emphasized earlier, reconciliation is constitutive to a people whose discipleship has made everything secondary to our primary commitment to the oneness of the body of Christ.

We sense that Disciples congregations are not drawing upon this covenant heritage as they could. It is, for example, a profound moment in the broken world we live in for us to declare each week around the Lord's table that his invitation is open to all, and that none of the divisions separating people in the world have sway around his table. It is our belief that any congregation that recognizes this is what it means in our time to stand on holy ground will itself experience the power of his transformative spirit each time it gathers at the table. Any congregational pastor can tell stories of visitors who are stunned by this open invitation to the table, an openness second nature to Disciples precisely because we know we are covenanted together by our commitment to Jesus as Lord. This is one of our major strengths, not only symbolized, but cemented each time we gather around the Lord's table.

Putting Covenant into Practice

There are ways to strengthen the sense of covenant in Disciples congregations. One practice some of our congregations have found helpful in claiming covenant as their way of life is the use of covenant pledges. Annual covenant renewal worship services during which the pledge is renewed collectively have also proven to be an effective way both to celebrate covenant making and to raise the consciousness level among the members of covenant's central role in their life together. Covenant is the cornerstone of genuine community. Because we have chosen to take the risk of letting covenant be the tie that bonds us together as a church, church members should be confident that their congregation is a welcoming and safe place for a diversity of people who are not sure church has a place for them anymore.

Another practice that is gaining momentum in our congregations is consensus decision-making. Most of our congregations live by majority rule. Robert's Rules of Order have become almost sacrosanct at every level of our church. This is unfortunate because it is counterproductive to strengthening a sense of covenantal life. Voting in churches is a "lose-lose" proposition, simply because it creates a "house divided against itself" church culture in which relationships become adversarial.

Despite the fact that on every level of Disciples life we have seen the negative effect of majority rule through voting, there remains a strong resistance to consensus decision-making as a viable alternative. Yet consensus decision-making has produced a stunning change in the culture of congregations that have tried it. What they report is that they had not previously understood the extent to which voting had created a negative environment for making decisions. They had lived in an adversarial church culture so long that they had become immune to its effects. But they also found that as negative as the impact of voting was on their congregations, reforming this practice was anything but easy.

However, because something is difficult does not mean it is not worth the effort. In this instance we believe what is at stake is too important to allow the status quo to go unchallenged. What is more, as difficult as moving to consensus decision-making may be, it is a rather simple process to implement. Once an item or issue is put before the church, views are shared as people feel led by the Spirit to speak, the goal of which is not to win support for one position or another, but to bring light to the discussion as the group searches to glimpse the will of God. After the time for people to speak has elapsed, the leader asks if there is a consensus for a particular action to be taken. If the group agrees there is, the decision is accepted. If someone doesn't agree, that person is asked if he or she has anything new to add to the discussion. If not, and in light of the obvious agreement among most present to take the action, the person is asked if she or he is willing to step aside, let the decision go forward, and support its implementation even without agreeing with it.

This kind of decision-making in a congregation does, of course, require a substantial degree of spiritual maturity. But the need for maturity can have the effect of calling it out of people, who do in fact rise to the level of expectations. It is entirely possible that the way most Disciples congregations make decisions is a de facto statement that they expect too little from their members, and that is what they get. The experience of Quaker congregations and even Quaker college and seminary faculties demonstrates that this process works, suggesting that it does come down to a question of will. We are convinced that if Disciples congregations have the will to try this way of making decisions, it will help them to reclaim their heritage as covenant communities of faith.

Communicating Who We Are

But as important as claiming our covenant tradition at the congregational level is, if a nation of people searching for genuine community are to experience it in Disciples congregations, they need to know we exist. A frequent comment some of our churches have heard from new members is that they didn't believe there was such a thing as a church that valued freedom of thought and also genuinely cared about one another. Such comments confirm what we have said among ourselves for too many years—that Disciples are the best kept secret in American religious life. There is little comfort in either reality. Most of our congregations can do better at making the kind of covenant community church they are known in the communities where they are located. It is not enough for people to know First Christian or Cedar Avenue Christian is in town. They need to know the kind of church these congregations are. This means that time, creativity, and money must be devoted to a concerted effort to make who they are known where they are.

One Disciples congregation decided to distribute business cards to the membership on which were printed an identifying statement about the kind of church it is, its name, its address, and its Web site. The purpose of the cards was for members to have something they could hand to another person with just enough information to make them want to go to the Web site for more details. They had already discovered that visitors who came because they already knew what kind of congregation they were were more likely to return than those who did not. In addition, the congregation placed special ads in the local newspaper large enough to draw attention, and these ads were very explicit in details about the kind of church they are. This church believes that being Disciples means it is not the kind of church everyone is looking for, but it is the kind that can attract people who want an open-minded approach to faith and a Communion table that excludes no one.

The Bible as Means Rather Than End

The second thing Disciples congregations can do to reclaim their identity is to teach the Bible as a means to an end rather than an end in itself. We have already underscored the fact that our founders believed scripture was central to the church's life, but they did not turn it into an idol that replaced Jesus as the focus of Christian devotion. The Bible was for them a source of inspiration and education. Moreover, having clergy and laity educated in the tools of interpretation were understood to be essential to the work of biblical study. Our founders believed in the freedom of all believers to read and understand the Bible only because they trusted that every Christian would desire to engage in this task. We think they would be both shocked and dismayed by the pervasive biblical illiteracy among Disciples. Yet this situation is an opportunity for who we are as a people to shine once again. In the next chapter we will focus on the necessary role clergy must play if this is to happen. Here we want to underscore what our personal experiences have taught us about the open-minded approach Disciples take to the Bible.

Put simply, people in our congregations love the Bible, although it is intimidating to many church members, in part because they don't possess sufficient knowledge about it to understand that it is accessible to them more than they believe. They have also heard opposite viewpoints on controversial issues such as abortion and homosexuality being justified by biblical quotes. But therein lies the opportunity for Disciples congregations to present an attractive alternative. While, as we have said, some Disciples believe in a literal interpretation of scripture, this has never been the only way we read the Bible, nor the dominant one. Disciples scholars have been leaders in historical critical study of the Bible. Congregations that embrace this approach to the message of scripture will likely be surprised at how receptive the majority of people will be to it. Most Christians come to the Bible with questions they want to explore. This fits well with the right of all Christians to read and interpret scripture for themselves, which has been a mark of who we are as Disciples.

At the same time, though, the open-minded approach to scripture that is the Disciples way calls for a change in congregational life that puts it in the forefront of what we do. The times in which we are living cry out for a radical commitment to serious Bible study. As we will argue in the next chapter, congregational pastors have been too busy with other tasks, neglecting their primary role as teacher of the faith. This simply has to change if Disciples congregations are to become places where new people encounter an environment in which questioning the Bible is considered a means of growth rather than a threat to faith.

Theology as Core to Congregational Life

What we are talking about in its broadest sense is a call for Disciples congregations to see themselves as theological centers. From the beginning of our movement Disciples have placed a premium on a well-informed faith. The fact that we have also allowed a wall of separation to grow between the academy and the congregation stands in contradistinction to this commitment. More true to who we are as a church would be a renewed focus in Disciples congregations on creating an environment of learning in which theology is the work all church members do to equip one another for ministry. As long as laity and clergy live in different theological worlds, the chance of congregational transformation is slight, not least because the major task transformation involves is the renewing of the mind.

Embracing Ecumenism

The ecumenical nature of Disciples life has often been left to those at the General and Regional levels of our church. Yet it may be that this part of our heritage can be a significant factor in transforming congregations that choose to highlight it. We say this because even though the general public may be postdenominational in attitude, sectarianism remains a debilitating problem in the Christian community. Christians who question traditional doctrines and beliefs are accustomed to having their discipleship questioned. One of our colleagues who publicly supported healthcare benefits for gay and lesbian state workers, to cite one example, was "rebuked in the name of Jesus" by a caller to his church.

There are Christians seeking a church home who do not subscribe to this kind of narrow thinking and who wonder if there are any congregations who also reject it. Here is an opportunity for Disciples congregations to make a statement about the kind of church we are. Sectarianism has been an anathema in our life together from the beginning. "Christians only, but not the only Christians" is more than a slogan for us. It is an essential element in our self-understanding. Being thoroughly Disciples at the congregational level means openly embracing this attitude in our words and actions. The now common practice of open membership in most of our congregations is testimony to our desire to practice what we preach. There is something quite inspiring about ecumenism at the local level as it teaches church members the practical benefits of unity without uniformity in their relationship to one another and members of other churches.

Yet a major obstacle to our ecumenical heritage having a major impact on congregational life is the tendency to think it is out of date, anachronistic, its day having passed. But the bitter sectarianism that characterizes American Christianity today is a direct challenge to this misguided thinking. As long as Christians use human doctrines and dogmas as tests of faith, there will be a place for spiritual maturity to show itself in an ecumenical witness that stands over against sectarianism. Disciples congregations have both the history and credibility to make this kind of witness. Michael has often said that the ecumenical movement has always been a church renewal movement. We want to take that a step further and suggest that ecumenism can in fact be transformative to congregations that consciously seek to embody it.

Lay-focused Mission

Mission is not auxiliary to the church; it is its lifeblood. This was the conviction behind the churchwide emphasis in the recent past on congregations writing mission statements. But there is no evidence that such statements effected any lasting change in the life of our churches. Mission on paper has not translated into missional action. We think one remedy to this problem is for congregations to begin making a conscious connection between mission and lay ministry. The mission of the church is an imperative for all Christians, lay and clergy, and is expressed in our varied calls and gifts. Disciples have always believed ministry is lay centered.

In spite of this heritage, church members have been conditioned to think their ministry is one of supporting the role of the clergy. This is both a theological and ecclesial problem. Practice has overwhelmed theology when it comes to the role of laity in the church. But even among those laity who have a solid biblical understanding of church and ministry, the structure of their congregation is likely to hinder any attempt they make to fulfill their calling. Indeed, calling and gift-evoking are concepts that have been corrupted to mean serving on committees and in elected offices. One of the realities of Disciples church life today we believe must be changed is the debilitating effect of the business model of organization found in the large majority of congregations. It is one of the ironies of Disciples life that the heirs of a movement whose founders wanted to use biblical words for biblical concepts are mired in a congregational structure that is so obviously unbiblical. Unless and until our congregations genuinely focus on call and gifts among the laity, transformation will be limited. We suggest that reclaiming the Disciples focus on the ministry of the laity can have a reforming effect on the way congregations organize themselves. The same need exists on the Regional and General Church levels as well, but it is possible that a change within congregations will form the basis for change in the other expressions of our church.

The Risk and Reward of Being Disciples

When the great handshake between the Christians of Kentucky and the Disciples of what is now Bethany, West Virginia, took place at Main Street Christian Church (now Central Christian Church) in Lexington in 1832, congregation was the only expression of church Disciples had. Since that time we have grown in understanding and practice, but our identity as a people, a movement, continues to bear witness to the congregation as the key to being a healthy church. All of us have a stake in the quality of congregational life among us. Our call for congregations to become consciously and boldly Disciples may sound ordinary, but we are convinced that such a step can have an extraordinary impact on the strength and quality of our churches. We would close with a story that makes us believe this is more than a hope.

Starting new Disciples congregation has been a major focus of our church over the last several years as we have sought to fulfill the challenge of the 20/20 Vision of starting a thousand new churches. Some of these efforts have gone well, others not. Some have taken off and grown quickly, while others have experienced a slow but steady growth. In at least one instance of which we are aware the new congregation has been of the latter type. Now firmly established, it has taken several years for it to get on its feet.

One of the pressures early on was for the clergy leadership of this new church to abandon the very principles of Disciples life we have articulated above. Many of the members had come from traditions that were creedal, doctrinal, and literal in their approach to the Bible. They chafed under the Disciples commitment to freedom of thought, especially in regard to moral issues. They found a historical approach to Bible study disturbing. They did not understand how our national church magazine could publish some of the articles it did on such issues. They wondered why the minister was willing to serve Communion to people whose sexual orientation led them to openly live in sin.

At the same time, a few members who had Disciples background began to affirm the position of the church's clergy leadership that whatever else the new church would be, it would be Disciples. They spoke of the fact that while they did not always agree with the minister, or the denomination, agreeing to disagree was core to what it meant to be who we are. It turned out to be a critical moment in this congregation's life. They lost people who could not be as Disciples as the congregation chose to be, but since that time it has grown into a vibrant community of faith because of the many more who have come and stayed because they like who Disciples are. We believe other new and established congregations in our church can have a similar experience. It is at the congregational level that Disciples identity is most important, not least because it is where the kind of church we are can have its most significant impact on the larger community. We believe the nature of Disciples life can fill the need today for genuine community because we are especially equipped to meet people where they are and love them into becoming so much more.

CHAPTER 9

Leadership

Pointing Direction, Sharing Responsibility

Disciples have traveled a circuitous path from Alexander Campbell calling ministers "hirelings" to having an order of ministry. Though Campbell's attitude toward clergy was not directed at clergy leadership as much as clericalism—i.e., the abusive authority of the ordained—his views have suffered from persistent misunderstanding that has produced an as-yet unresolved historic tension between laity and clergy in our tradition.

Core Principles

It was no surprise that the order of ministry that Disciples now recognize emerged incrementally and quietly after Restructure. At issue was how such an order fit into our core commitment to the ministry of the laity. From the beginning of our movement, lay ministry has never been simply a good idea, but fundamental to what we believe about the Holy Spirit empowering all Christians to do ministry (Acts 2).

Another reason for the caution with which Disciples developed an order of ministry was our longstanding suspicion of the place of bishops in the life of the church. Disciples had never accepted the argument for apostolic succession, but some of our lay and clergy leaders wondered if an order of ministry was laying the foundation for acceptance of it to remove an obstacle to our participation in a united church

Both these principles seem to play a prominent role in the recent statement of the Lexington Seminary faculty in response to the Churches Uniting in Christ document on Mutual Recognition and Mutual Reconciliation of Ministries. They minced no words in criticizing the document's presumption that bishops are responsible "for maintaining the apostolicity and unity of the worship and sacramental life of the church."[1] Accepting the document's position, they said, would mean Disciples would be required to abandon the historic practice of lay participation in ministerial functions such as baptism or presiding at the Communion table, thereby, creating a hierarchy of ministry that contradicts everything we have believed and practiced regarding the church's ministry.

Both of the authors of this book affirm the Disciples tradition of lay ministry, but we also think this statement by some of our former colleagues suggests they are locked in old concepts that led them to misinterpret what the Churches Uniting document was actually saying. Our understanding of the document is that it does not require ordained clergy to preside at the table and does not speak in hierarchical terms, even as it affirms bishops in apostolic succession. Instead, it uses the imagery of concentric circles with bishops or those not called as such, with the responsibility of teaching the faith.

Disciples Contributions to Discussions on Lay and Professional Ministry

Our disagreement with the Lexington faculty statement serves as an example of the kind of rigorous debates Disciples have had on leadership throughout our history, and is why we think our church has much to contribute to the ongoing discussion among denominations as they seek to reconcile their ministries. At the same time, more work within our own household of faith is needed to strengthen the ministry of both laity and clergy. The two are inextricably intertwined among Disciples to the point that the weakness of one undercuts the healthiness of the other. This is why the tendency to emphasize lay ministry at the congregational level by diminishing the leadership role of clergy is misguided. The Disciples' historic focus on lay ministry was not intended to create a competitive relationship with clergy. Yet such a competitive relationship exists, and in some instances even in the attitude of clergy, suggesting that lingering effects of Alexander Campbell's ambiguous attitude about ministers remain.

Equally detrimental to both lay and clergy leadership is the persistent image of the minister as the church's version of a CEO. We see this attitude at all levels of church among Disciples. It is pervasive enough at the congregational level that clergy leadership could be characterized as facing the challenge of producing tangible results for the church members "(stockholders)", measured by attendance (customers) and offerings (sales figures). In addition, the sole purpose of lay ministry becomes one of filling slots in the organizational chart to help the ministerial staff accomplish the above stated goals. This is a bit of a parody, of course, but it is close enough to the truth to warrant a serious assessment of the function of both clergy and lay leadership.

Ministerial Functions among Disciples

The Need for Clergy Leadership

Perhaps a place to start is to state the obvious. Disciples have an urgent need for good clergy leadership because it holds the key to evoking the ministry of the laity. Once during a meeting of the Lexington Theological Seminary faculty, the issue of a shortage of Disciples ministers came up. Then-President William Paulsell responded that the church has always had a shortage of *good* ministers. Perhaps the comment was a bit tongue in cheek, but it at least underscored the fact that developing capable ministerial leadership is an ongoing need among Disciples. As we shall see, competent clergy do not diminish lay ministry. They strengthen it.

Ministry as "In Christ's Place"

One voice from our past to which we would do well to appeal again as we think about leadership today is that of Disciples historian Ronald Osborn. He, better than most, eloquently captured the core of what Disciples believe about the responsibility of all Christians, especially clergy, when he described ministry as serving "where Christ is, in Christ's place."[2] Osborn said that Christ "came as a Servant...to make known the forgiving love of God for the whole world," so the church is called to the same ministry.[3] While he was writing about the ordained ministry, he would have been the first to say that his metaphor applies to clergy and laity, and stands firmly in the Disciples tradition in affirming the rightful place of clergy in the church's ministry without creating a hierarchical system. This is especially the case since serving in Christ's place was a way of reminding the church and its ministers that all ministry is given. We do Christ's ministry. We continue what was God's initiative in Jesus Christ. For the church as a whole and the ordained in particular, this means that in the midst of our human frailty we are given a holy vocation.

Ronald Osborn's description of ministry as serving in Christ's place has proven to be of lasting value as Disciples have worked on developing good leaders in the intervening years since his book was published.

Interestingly enough, his view of ministry has striking parallels with several things John Gardner says about leadership. Gardner delivered a series of lectures on leadership sponsored by the Independent Sector, a nonprofit coalition of over 600 foundation, corporate, and voluntary organization members. Gardner was one of the most astute civic and government leaders of the twentieth century. He served as president of the Carnegie Corporation and the Carnegie Foundation for the Advancement of Teaching as well as being Secretary of Health, Education, and Welfare under Lyndon Johnson. He could have been talking about the church—even Disciples—when he noted that too many segments of American society seem to believe good leadership will emerge if we talk about it long enough. Gardner makes a more positive point that relates to the way Disciples think about leadership: "Most of our leaders are followers in other contexts, and followers often perform leader-like acts."[4] In the church we speak of this fact in terms of everyone being a leader at the point of his or her gift, and a follower at the point of the gifts of others. The point is that leadership is a two-way street and must be mutually beneficial.

Equipping Laity for Ministry

For Disciples the point at which this mutual benefit becomes most urgent is in the equipping of laity for ministry. Alexander Campbell believed laity could and would lead the church as long as they were equipped biblically and theologically to do so. His vision remains elusive primarily because the Disciples version of equipping is a lay-led Sunday school class or a sporadic clergy led Bible study that has no curriculum order to it. If this pattern is to change, a fundamental reform in the way we think about the nature of congregational life will be necessary.

Recovering the Synagogue Concept

Building on what we have already said about Disciples congregations in the previous chapter, we suggest that a basic need is for us to recover the concept of "synagogue." In the rabbinical tradition, the synagogue is the place of instruction in the Torah, where people learn their story and law, both of which are what make the Torah what it is. We think this is a model for Christian congregational life. Specifically, congregations need to become miniature theological seminaries where the primary focus is on study. Clergy should serve as the faculty, whether it be a single-pastor congregation or a multiple staff one, because teaching is our major responsibility. We are called to be the resident theologians. Other tasks such as administration, counseling, and pastoral visitation have a place, but if we want to see genuine congregational transformation as we say we do, these other tasks can no longer be permitted to take the place of the equipping of the laity for ministry through teaching.

The Christian story should be on the lips of every church member who can speak about the life and teachings of Jesus, his death, and his resurrection with competence and confidence. What is more, historical criticism that lies at the core of seminary education today should not be a foreign subject to laypeople. The freedom to interpret scripture for ourselves promoted by our founders presumed a thorough knowledge of the Bible. Yet the opposite is the case today. Biblical literacy among church members is not high, and certainly not where it can be. The distinction taught in seminary between what the biblical writer meant and what a text means today is news to many laypeople, as is the fact that an English translation is itself an interpretation based on partial manuscripts because no original texts are extant.

The Clergy's Teaching Role

Disciples clergy urgently need to reclaim the central teaching role if we hope to avoid the gospel becoming ever more irrelevant in people's daily life. If the challenge is to know how to live the Christian life in the modern world, as Bonhoeffer suggested, it will not be met without a conscious effort to create a synagogue environment in our congregations. This is because theology matters, a fact about which all churches, including Disciples, have often been quite casual. As University of Virginia professor Charles Marsh puts it:

Theology matters now more than ever, and it will not do to wish that [theologians] go away... The theologian needs to be heard in the public conversation on religion and politics and by pastors and laity in churches... Too many of us in the Christian community have forgotten that we stand in a tradition of careful thinking and articulation, that there are intellectual demands that come in confessing Christ, rules of speech and reasoning. At its best, theology has a way of slowing down language, interrupting easy formulas, unsettling partisan confidences, and disciplining thought. Can anyone doubt that the churches in the United States could use a little more theology and a lot less religious talk?[5]

Because theology matters, teaching must once again become the primary responsibility of clergy. What is more, competent lay leadership depends on it. The theological education ministers receive to become good leaders must be passed on to laity. This is why congregations beginning to function as synagogues, or communities of learning, is an urgent need.

Theology and Transformational Leadership

Disciples speak often these days about "transformation." Such talk will come to naught or lead us in the wrong direction unless it is grounded in theological reflection. We are hopeful that the reason we are talking so much about transformation is because deep inside our collective spirit as a church we know intuitively that Disciples life needs more than renewal of old ways.

Discomfort with the Status Quo

The New Testament term for transformation is "metamorphosis" (Rom. 12:2), which underscores that the kind of change the Spirit of God effects is not small. Old ways have the power to condition us to accept what is as if it is all there can be. Gardner says that leaders in fact become comfortable with the status quo that rewards them for not rocking the boat. "Young leaders," he says, "become 'servants of what is' rather than 'shapers of what might be.'"[6] He further writes:

> In the long process of learning how the system works, [young leaders] are rewarded for playing within the intricate structures of existing rules and the hierarchy it has created; they think in terms of reaching the top rung of the ladder of success only to find they have become prisoners of the structure. In one sense this is not all bad since every vital system reaffirms itself. But no system can stay vital for long unless some of its leaders remain sufficiently independent to help it change and grow.[7]

Facing Opposition to Change

We have already alluded to the fact that anyone who has been in the church for more than a day knows that the church doesn't usually respond in a positive way to leaders who call for change. More often, it resists those leaders and may even condemn them—either openly or behind the scenes. Disciples leaders who have dared to challenge existing structures have encountered institutional resistance that has sought to marginalize their influence. Thus, cronyism often becomes the modus operandi for the process by which Disciples gather leaders, whatever manifestation of church we are talking about. Even efforts to create racial and gender balance fall into this trap, with the same people filling various positions of leadership year after year. The church often acts as if it fears the independent leader who is committed to the healthiness of the church, but who also refuses to accept the status quo without questioning its effectiveness.

Disciples' Need for Transformationalists

Disciples need this kind of leader, most especially if we are truly serious about all our talk about transformation. Transformational leaders, what Gardner calls "transformationalists," are those who can discern the practices that continue to serve us effectively and those needing to be reformed or eliminated. Gardner says such leaders know how to balance continuity and change to preserve the deepest values with which the group began as it is adjusting to new circumstances.[8] Institutional stability does not depend on keeping things the way they've always been. It rests, instead, on the ability of leaders to make the right kinds of changes at the right moment. It is Christ, not the church, who scripture says remains the same yesterday, today, and tomorrow (Heb. 13:8). The church is transitory, and should be alert to ways it can and must adapt to changing needs and circumstances.

Leading from Within

Parker Palmer says that leaders who can guide the church into and through transformation decision-making are people who "lead from within." This, he says, is how leaders shape external realities born of the spiritual traditions of which they are a part. If our faith has taught us anything, he suggests, it is that "external reality does not impinge upon us as a prison or an ultimate constraint...that we co-create the world, that we live in and through a complex interaction of what is inside of us and what is 'out there.'"[9] In fact, he says, it is our very spiritual tradition that leads us to believe that we create the reality of the outer world by projecting our spirit on it.[10] Spirituality, then, is not about values and ethics. It is, instead, he says, about what we project onto the external world. We will project either a spirit of light or a spirit of shadow, a spirit of hope or a spirit of despair. In either case, we will become co-creators of the external world. How we do this is a choice all of us make.[11] Yet what Palmer says should be understood within the context of the larger task of our seeking to discern the will of God. The goal of such seeking is to embody the divine will in and through our lives, a process that is best done in community.

Being co-creators with God is not a strange concept to Disciples. Our long-standing commitment to justice seeking is an example of how we are working to bring order to chaos in the external world. Too often, though, this passion has led to actions that have not necessarily arisen from within, but have been responses shaped by the outward situation. What leading from within suggests is that a more effective way to act in the world is to follow our discernment of the leading of the Spirit in community with others.

Listening for Decisions

At the same time, leading from within invites Disciples clergy to begin the spiritual practice of listening for decisions rather than "making" them. This is a perspective developed by Sister Elaine Prevalett. "If we believe, as we say we do," she writes, "that God's Spirit dwells in each of us; if we believe, as we say we do, that we are all members of one Body, and that each of us is gifted in his or her own way with a certain role to play, it makes sense to believe that that Indwelling Spirit will give us the nudges we need."[12] Listening for decision depends on our discernment of those nudges, born of the experience of "some modicum of quiet, especially inner quiet...a developed prayer life...[and] the capacity to act out of something other than our heads."[13] Sister Elaine is not naïve about how difficult this way of leading is for Westerners who are rational, extraverted, and action oriented. Nonetheless, she is convinced that cutting away the excesses of our daily lives to a life of genuine simplicity is possible, and when we do, we will make better decisions.

Obviously, as she suggests, leading from within requires self-discipline if we are going to engage the spiritual practices that have proven indispensable. Experience has left little doubt that such self-discipline is irregular and sporadic. Just as we talk about losing weight more than actually doing it, we who lead in the church often find that we talk about going spiritually deeper much more than we experience the spiritual depths. The call to lead from within will likely not transform the way church leaders lead immediately, but too much is at stake to accept things as they now exist. The potential for change is enormous because we have many capable leaders who can be the kind of "transformationalists" we need. While we may always have a shortage of good ministers, lay and clergy alike, we have a sufficient number to effect a churchwide transformation of Disciples life.

Prophetic Witness: The Task of Pointing Direction

We want to highlight one last dimension of transformational leadership, even though by its nature it carries with it a potential of creating tension within congregations and denominations. These leaders offer a prophetic witness to the church, focusing on the temptations the church faces to compromise faithfulness to the gospel. While laity may exercise this kind of leadership, we are thinking primarily of prophetic witness in regard to the role of clergy in equipping laity. In this regard, we do not understand prophetic ministry as railing against the sins of the people, though our sins are ever before us. Rather, we are thinking in terms of having the capacity to point direction.

This leadership quality is what Robert Greenleaf says constitutes the core of servant leadership. More than any twentieth-century writer, Greenleaf brought servant leadership to the forefront of church thinking, even though he spent his career in the secular world as essentially a paid thinker for AT&T as well as a teacher at MIT and Harvard. His vocation, however, was Christian service as a dedicated Quaker. Greenleaf said good leaders are able to point direction better than most through a capacity for "penetrating insight" expressed in a compelling vision.[14] For him, leading meant going out ahead to show the way, rather than guiding, directing, managing, or administering, terms he said "imply either maintenance (keeping things going as they are), or coercion (sanctions or implied threat of sanctions to enforce one's will), or manipulation (guiding others into thoughts or actions that they may not fully understand)."[15] Greenleaf considered the roles of the prophet, seeker, and leader as inextricably linked. For this reason he argued that a good leader could not lead without faithful seekers who were ready and willing to move in a new direction,[16] familiar counsel to Disciples whose entire history has been one of emphasizing the collective ministry of clergy and lay.

Pointing direction, then, is a call to Disciples clergy to lead the church by stepping out front in words and actions that may challenge the status quo within the church when it begins to look more like the world than the kingdom of God. This kind of ministerial leadership highlights the responsibility seminaries have in educating leaders who have the capacity and will to lead in this way. Obviously, clergy cannot lead laity where they do not want to go, but neither are laity likely to take actions to which no one is pointing. Here Disciples clergy have something on which to build. Throughout our history we as a people have shown the will to be more faithful in practicing justice within our own household. Moreover, as Greenleaf also said, prophetic leadership does not contradict the role of church leaders to nurture people in faith and to build trust for God and one another. It is constitutive to it. The key, he said, is having church members who are seeking faithfulness enough to test the authenticity of what the prophet minister is saying.[17]

Summary: Clergy and Laity in Partnership

This brings us back to where we started. Clergy and lay ministry are partners in leadership. The one needs the other, and the church needs both. Since our founding, Disciples have said we believe this, yet we have also shown a tendency to slip into patterns of thinking and practice that move us in the opposite direction. Perhaps we have always faced a shortage of good ministers. If so, the challenge and the opportunity we have in this new century is to ensure that this will not be our story in the future. With all manifestations of our church life working to this end, the future can become now.

As a people we have labored to hold on to a vision of church that is both local and universal. What we need now are lay and clergy leaders who are willing to think boldly and provocatively to move Disciples life outside the church box we have constructed for ourselves. The axiom "To keep doing what you're doing will keep giving you what you've got" is true; only we can add, "To keep thinking the same things you've always thought will give you the same old ideas." Perhaps C.S. Lewis said it best when he commented, "If you've taken a wrong turn, then to keep going in the direction you're going gets you no nearer to where you want to be." To keep thinking and doing what we've been thinking and doing while expecting different results is to keep traveling the road we're on that will not take us to where we want to be. We are being called to a new land, and the old paths will not get us there. We have tried new marketing techniques, new renewal programs, and advice from consultants without changing our way of thinking about what it means to be church and to do ministry in the world of today. A new way is the only way that can take us to where we want to be, but without a theologically informed leadership, that way will remain elusive.

CHAPTER 10

Being Disciples in the Twenty-first Century

A Story We Can Tell

In each of the chapters of this book, we have sought to clarify our identity in order to have a basis for examining our actions and for offering suggestions for ways they can be reformed. We recognize that our polity makes achieving consensus on identity and practice difficult. At the same time, we think we have shown that Disciples do in fact have a story to tell that reveals strands of thoughts and actions that have been consistent and persistent enough to form us into a particular people: We believe we are Christians only but not the only Christians; we believe unity and diversity coexist; we believe the biblical message is accessible to all who desire to study it; we take statements of faith seriously without insisting they define the content of the Christian gospel for everyone; we believe no one has the right to judge the worthiness of another who professes commitment to the Lordship of Jesus; we come to the Communion table at the Lord's invitation, not the church's; we believe outward symbols can witness to inward transformation, chief among them baptism; we believe in the ministry of all Christians while ordaining and licensing some who have been called to the more specialized task of teaching and preaching the Word; we understand that we can do together many things none of us can do alone; we believe the visible unity of the church is constitutive of a credible witness to the love of God revealed in Jesus Christ.

A Big Tent Church

We think the above statements describe who Disciples are in much the same way as the principles the Vision Team has developed to explain the identity statement, "We are Disciples of Christ, a movement for wholeness in a fragmented world. As part of the one body of Christ, we welcome all to the Lord's table as God has welcomed us." Both our statements and theirs attest to Disciples being a "big tent" church, open to all who claim the name of Jesus.

The Challenge Today

We believe this identity that has sustained us throughout our history can continue to do so as we move deeper into the twenty-first century. But as we have argued, changes in practice are needed. Obviously we are not alone in our thinking. When the General Board appointed the Mission Alignment Coordinating Council in April of 2008, it charged the Council with the task of leading our denomination "in imagining a church organized around our stated mission priorities." As a reminder, those priorities are: becoming a Pro-reconciling/ Anti-racist church; formation of 1,000 new congregations by 2020; transformation of 1,000 current congregations by 2020; leadership development necessary to realize these new and renewed congregations.

Two Basic Questions

Whatever the end results of the MACC turn out to be, the least that can be said is that the Council reflects the fact that there is growing support for changing the way our church functions. Our concern is that any changes be consistent with our historic identity. Denominational identity can never be taken for granted. It can be lost easily as later generations seek to put into practice general beliefs and principles whose meaning must be interpreted in light of a given historical context. For example, we may agree that Disciples believe the Communion table is the Lord's table, not ours, but does that mean we are ready to welcome all regardless of race, nationality, theology, or sexual orientation? We affirm the right of all Christians to think for themselves, but does that truly apply to the way we read the Bible? We are an ecumenical church that believes division in the body of Christ is an anathema to the gospel, but how far are we willing to bend in our practices to be a part of Churches Uniting in Christ?

To some among us the answers to all these questions are obvious, while to just as many they are not at all. As much as we may talk about diversity, it is one of the most difficult practices communities of faith face. Common sense would tell us that there are limits to tolerance. But what are they and who gets to set them?

This book is our attempt to provide some guidance in answering that question. We understand the limitations of our work and do not entertain any illusions about quick agreement or acceptance of our suggestions. The modest goal we have is to contribute to the current discussions swirling around identity and practice, and perhaps to broaden the participation, especially at the congregational level. We believe it is essential for Disciples laity to engage the great issues we are facing as we move into the future. The chapter on congregational life was intended to point in this direction. Now we want to focus on the General and Regional manifestations of Disciples life, knowing that what is done at either level will necessarily be in relationship to and with congregations.

It seems to us that the work being done in the General Church and in some Regions is an attempt to answer two fundamental questions: (1) What kind of church do we need to be to express who we are as a people; and (2) What are we who are part of this church willing to do to build it up? We think these questions go to the heart of what we are trying to do denominationally as we work to stabilize our life in order to fulfill the mission to which we have committed ourselves. To this end we want to conclude this work with a discussion, albeit brief, of some of the more troubling issues up to this point that we have not addressed in a direct way. We think Disciples simply must find some common ground on these issues if the future is to be worthy of our past.

What Kind of Church Do We Need to Be to Express Who We Are as a People?

Ordaining Homosexual Candidates

The first issue is the ordination of openly homosexual candidates for ministry. At the moment practices vary from Region to Region. A few Regions ordain gays and lesbians, but most do not. Most unsettling is that some Regions have adopted a de facto "don't ask, don't tell" practice that we think has the potential for undermining the integrity of the ordination process. In some instances Regions that do not ordain openly homosexual candidates will nonetheless grant them yearly standing, which certifies them to serve in ministry. In some respects this has encouraged commissions on ministry to practice "don't ask, don't tell" when it comes to ordination. We see this practice as a backdoor way for the Regions to circumvent a policy with which they disagree.

If it is not unseemly for the church to be playing this kind of game, and we think it is, it is at least a potential powder keg. Worse, it displays a failure to be a people who have the courage of their convictions. Those of us who believe sexual orientation should not be a factor in ordination qualifications should be willing to make the case openly for such a policy, and be willing to live with the consequences for making this witness. The authors of this book believe the argument in favor of ordaining openly homosexual persons who are otherwise qualified is a strong one, not least because we are a church whose historic position on discipleship is that we accept a person's profession of faith at face value. No one gets to judge the sincerity of another. This principle should apply to the process for ordination, especially with research clearly on the side of homosexuality not being a choice, but a genetic predisposition.

Can Disciples have a civil discussion on the practice we are suggesting? Of course we can, as long as covenant is a priority to us. Two possible solutions we think are worthy of consideration have the potential for preserving our identity and unity as a church. The first is an action taken by the Regional Assembly of the Upper Midwest Region in the fall of 2008 that replaced a policy that explicitly prohibited the ordination of gays and lesbians. The new policy states that it is the responsibility of congregations to recommend candidates for ordination to the Regional Commission on Ministry, regardless of sexual orientation. It further says that once a person receives congregational endorsement, final approval for ordination by the Commission will be based on qualifications, without concern for sexual orientation. At the same time, the proposal also affirms the fact that congregations continue to have exclusive right of call in regard to clergy leadership. What we think is especially encouraging about this action is that after extensive floor debate, it passed by a two to one margin.

A second approach we wish to offer is to move ordination guidelines away from Regions to the General Church level, specifically, the office of General Minister and President. The reasons our practices are varied and at times contradictory is because each Region determines an ordination policy for itself. We think guidelines should become a national standard. The General Minister and President is the person to work collaboratively with other parts of our church to formulate such a standard that can be presented to the General Board for approval. In this way qualifications for ministry become consistent for all Disciples. Regions will continue to nurture ordination candidates and make final decisions regarding approval, as well as making assessments related to standing. Moreover, congregations will retain the right of call. Our proposal, therefore, protects the responsibilities that now exist while creating a uniform guideline for ordination. It is, we believe, a way for Disciples to witness to the unity of the church through its ordination process.

Licensed Lay Ministers

Licensed lay ministry has been a part of Disciples life for many years, but with more congregations unable to afford a full-time minister, its ranks have grown. As of this writing, there are discussions at the General Church level to revise the Order of Ministry in ways that will include making licensure equivalent to ordination. Whatever any future decision about this might be, it is clear that a pressing need in our church is to make licensed ministry uniform in terms of requirements, especially educational. At the present time laypeople with extensive theological study and those with virtually none are being licensed. We would argue that no one should be sanctioned by the church for ministry without adequate theological training. The demands and responsibilities of modern-day ministry are too great for anything less. One way this challenge can be met is for Regions to draw on the expertise and skills of ordained ministers to serve as "teachers" for those seeking licensure. There are more than enough good minds among us to put flesh on this idea, with the hope and expectation that it will benefit the whole church if we do.

Financial Resources

Third, we must reform the way we receive and distribute financial resources in a way that recommits us to being one church. Disciples once boasted of the development of unified promotions as a symbol of our common bond in funding all the ministries of our church. At the moment, funding is in a state of disarray, indicative, we think, of the extent to which a commitment to covenant has diminished in the face of concerns for survival. What we apparently have forgotten as a church is that healthiness and suffering are collective experiences. One Region suffering means all Regions suffer. One Unit prospering while another weakens affects the whole church. Each Region and Unit needs to be concerned about all Regions and Units. Funding must become an expression of this commitment. Again, we believe the General Minister and General Board together should be where this issue is settled. We do not lack creative solutions to accomplish this task. We lack the will. In the past leaders sacrificed for the common good. That same spirit will have to guide us if we hope to extricate ourselves from funding chaos.

New Congregational Identity

Another reform in practice needed to make a statement about the kind of church we are has to do with the 20/20 Vision priority of establishing 1,000 new congregations. It is a worthy goal that has been in the forefront of our common life for the last several years. The work done thus far has been a source of encouragement and pride for Disciples. But the issue of identity continues to be something to which we think too little attention has been given. Are new congregations embracing the *muthos* (story) and *ethos* (ethic) that are historically Disciples'? This is a legitimate question to be asked. Our congregations are diverse in numerous ways, but, as we have argued, diversity should not be construed to suggest Disciples have no shared identity. The question is not uniformity. It is identity. Just as the authors of this book believe congregational transformation can flourish in churches that reclaim the core elements of being Disciples, we believe new congregations that do the same will see their foundations grow firm.

Part of the task in maintaining Disciples identity is for Regions to have programs that educate clergy and congregations new to Disciples on our history, identity, and polity. Moreover, we think national standards for this purpose could be very beneficial. At the moment the practice is varied and uneven. It is possible in some Regions for a minister and congregation to be accepted into the Disciples fold long before they are familiar with what makes us who we are as a church. We believe this is unadvisable and should be changed. The responsible way is to have a candidacy stage, during which the minister and congregation will go through the educational and relational process we are suggesting before full acceptance is granted.

The Office of General Minister and President

The *Design* of our church established the position of General Minister and President (GMP) as if the person would be the leader of our church, but it structured the office in a way that made it nearly impossible for this to become a reality. The ministry of the General Church is carried out through the Units, yet the GMP has no authority and little influence on the Units' decision-making. They have their own presidents and boards. When the General Minister speaks, our church listens, and then does what it wants to. An exaggerated statement to be sure, but closer to the way we function than some would admit.

We propose that the office of General Minister and President be entrusted with more responsibility than it now has. One example of this is to bring the implementation of the four priorities of the 20/20 Vision under the GMP's office, as well as all future ones we hope will be forthcoming from the 2009 General Assembly (see chapter 1) and succeeding ones. The good work Church Extension is doing in both new church establishment and congregational transformation notwithstanding, we believe churchwide priorities should be the responsibility of the GMP. Only the GMP is elected by the General Assembly and is, therefore, accountable to the whole church. It strikes us as strange that the funding agency of our church would be responsible for new church establishment and transforming congregations rather than the GMP.

We can also envision a structure whereby all the General Units of the church would become ministries functioning under the General Board, with the GMP serving as the head of a General Church staff composed of Unit presidents who would continue to have primary responsibility for their respective ministries.

The point of our proposal is to bring attention to the need at this point in our history for leadership at the highest level of our denomination to be one called by the whole church to speak for the whole church in words and in practice. Responsibility and funding need to be delegated to our GMP whenever the church approves a priority it wants implemented on behalf of the whole church.

The Future of Seminaries

Disciples have been committed to an educated clergy and laity since the beginning. Through the years we have established colleges and seminaries second to none in the quality of education they provide. In regard to the latter, however, we suggest the future will require our church to give serious thought to its ability to continue to maintain the four freestanding seminaries—Lexington, Christian, and Phillips Theological Seminaries, and Brite Divinity School. Each of these institutions has superb faculties who provide an essential service to Disciples and other denominations in the education of clergy. But resources are limited in a denomination our size, and these schools are struggling to maintain financial stability. We realize that each of these seminaries receives support from sources outside Disciples, but their histories show that through the years they have received their major funding from dedicated Disciples clergy and laity. We believe the time is not far into the future when a question of the stewardship of these resources will require both the seminaries and our church to ask if merger is a possible solution to limited and in some instances declining resources. At this point we raise this issue only as a way to suggest that it may be time to think creatively about ways we can continue to be faithful to our historic commitment to theological education rather than to wait until financial circumstances force us into decisions we have not had time to think through.

The Shape and Role of Regions

A sixth issue we think needs to be addressed is how to reshape Regions to establish an unequivocal identity and function for them. Currently most Regions are still facing financial shortfalls that have led to staff and program reductions. Our position is that this is a symptom rather than the problem. The fundamental issue is that Regions lack a clear purpose. We know what they do, but that's not the same as defining who they are. We suggest this dilemma begins with Regional ministers themselves. They wear labels such as "Regional Pastor," "General Minister and President," "Regional Minister," and others. What does this say about who they are in our church or who the rest of us understand them to be? What kind of authority do they have, or should they have? Disciples do not have bishops or show any sign of wanting to move in this direction. Does this mean Regional ministers serve primarily as administrators? If so, is this work that could be done by qualified laypeople?

All of us bear responsibility for the struggles Regions are experiencing, but to continue to believe Regions are viable in their current state only postpones the inevitable implosion that will happen if things continue in the direction they are now going. In this brief space we cannot exhaust all the issues that pertain to Regional restructuring, but we can make a start. So this is our proposal.

First, we state the obvious at the Regional level. While the church as the body of Christ exists in whatever form and whenever it gathers, its continuing institutional expression here on earth is congregational. Because of the nature of congregational polity, Disciples are a bottom-up institution. This is a crucial fact in understanding the role of Regions. The most functionally sound definition of a Region is that it is a collective expression of congregational life in a given geographical area. This means a Region exists only when congregations express a collective will for it. It has no reason to exist apart from the congregations that constitute it.

Second, the collective will arises from the perceived need for communication among the congregations about common concerns, goals, and needs. A practical way for this to work could be an annual gathering of congregational representatives who come together to worship and to work to develop the mission imperatives for a given Region. Such a gathering would replace the traditional Regional Assembly as we now know it. Gone would be outside speakers who offer a moment's inspiration but no long-term benefit. Most of the time would be spent in working groups followed by plenary sessions. Important to this process would be decision-making by consensus so that voting could not be used to divide the congregations one from the other.

A significant difference in these mission goals from what we are doing now is that they would be limited to what smaller groupings of congregations want to do in their geographical locations. In other words, the working groups would be organized along geographical areas within a Region. Each group would be charged with discerning what it wants to do in mission together and then to propose that to the other working groups to gain their support in prayer and financing.

The role of the Regional minister(s) then becomes fourfold: (1) traveling the Region speaking in congregations to articulate the mission goals of all the areas of the Region as a cause for mutual support; (2) raising funds for these missions; (3) facilitating each area's achieving its stated mission goals through guidance, counsel, and research; (4) assist congregations in search and call. These functions make large Regional staffs unnecessary, because they eliminate a large portion of programming that once characterized Regional ministry. Financial restraints have, of course, already forced many Regions to reduce positions, but this is a reactive response. What we are proposing is proactive, making smaller staffs desirable rather than reluctant realities.

Our proposal is intended to be as much provocative as exhaustive. Regions need to become much more engaged in opening the door to a wide range of possibilities as they discuss adapting to changing circumstances in the church. A deterrent to this work continues to be the tendency of Regions to measure their effectiveness by Disciples Mission Fund giving or the number of new congregations started. We see this practice as a sign of business as usual, not least because it fails to understand that many congregations practice covenant in their DMF funding but also view Regional and General Church leadership as unable to lead in the ways that are needed. If the church is about relationships, then the quality of the relationship between all three manifestations of Disciples life is how we can measure the healthiness of our common life as a church.

What Are We Willing to Do to Contribute to Building up This Kind of Church?

The above discussion ultimately brings us to a second question, "What are we willing to do to help build up this kind of church?" As important and urgent as any issue our church faces, the real impact it will have on Disciples as a whole depends on the extent to which we are willing to do what it takes to work on behalf of our denomination as it tries to put its words into actions.

The old adage that says there's no free lunch could not be truer than when it comes to the kind of church we want to be. As living organisms, churches grow and change according to the influence of their members. The way a congregation grows and what it becomes are the result of what all its members are willing to contribute to that end. Good church life doesn't just happen. It takes effort. Any member truly active in a church finds no neutral ground. Each is a member of a living body with something to contribute to its health and well-being.

Disciples often view church membership in an individualistic way. We talk about unity, but we so often consider ourselves lone ranger Christians. Our role in the church is considered a matter of personal discretion. Attendance, financial support, engagement in prayer, participation in ministry, growth in knowledge and understanding of scripture and church history, or thoughtful reflection on contemporary issues, all of these are personal decisions alone. This way of thinking is consistent with the significant influence on us as a church of John Locke's philosophy regarding the autonomy of the individual. What our founders overlooked is that Locke's thinking contradicts the core understanding among Disciples that we belong to the body of Christ. For too many among us, community consciousness is dwarfed by individualism. The impact of one person's behavior on others is seldom considered. When asked directly if they value their tradition, these people will answer in the affirmative. Yet they do as little as possible to make us stronger, and sometimes work in ways that weaken us. Dissent and disagreement are never a problem when they occur in discussions of people who share a commitment to the well-being of the whole.

What is needed is for all of us to realize that in practice, being Disciples depends on the degree to which we are willing to contribute to our common life together. This translates into two tangible commitments: (1) participation and (2) financial support. Words mean little unless they are spoken by those who are working on behalf of the good of the whole. Regions and the General Church need the prayers, presence, and hard work of all of us to be effective in their ministries. Congregations need the same from Regions and the General Church. There are numerous ways we can be together for worship and service, and we think every person in our church bears the responsibility to determine how he or she can make this offering.

In regard to the financial support of the church, we make this proposal. Individual congregational support for the Disciples Mission Fund, no matter how inadequate it may be at the moment in its structure and function, should not be affected by agreement or disagreement over actions and policies. That is to say, what congregations give should be based on their desire to support the church, not on whether or not they agree with the decisions being made by the larger church. We realize this calls for a high level of spiritual maturity, but we are willing to trust that it is present more than we might think. We have acknowledged that one of the ways congregations have expressed their discontent with the direction of our church has been by withdrawing financial support. But we believe this runs counter to the nature of the church as the body of Christ. It not only does damage to the Regional and General Church expressions of our church. It also hurts congregational life. A house divided against itself in any form undercuts the foundations of that house.

This proposal is not suggesting that congregations and individuals across our denomination cannot or should not question decisions being made or priorities being followed. Rather, we are saying that this can be done through the first commitment we discussed—participation in the life of the church. Involvement is the key to reforming practices, changing direction, forging new ministries. Uninterrupted financial support can be a sign of devotion to the future health and well-being of our denomination even as we discuss and debate how to move into that future. "Joined together in Discipleship" is not just a phrase about us. It is who we are, and should shape everything we do.

Notes

Preface

[1]See "The U.S. Religious Landscape Survey Reveals a Fluid and Diverse Pattern of Faith," at http://pewforum.org, posted February 25, 2008.

[2]Robert Wuthnow, *Christianity in the 21st Century* (New York: Oxford Univ. Press, 1993), 51.

Chapter 1: Why We Are Disciples

[1]These are available through www.disciples.org/21stCenturyVisionTeam/tabid/335/Default.aspx.

[2]*Program of the International Centennial Celebration and Conventions of the Disciples of Christ* (Cincinnati: American Christian Missionary Society, 1909), 11.

[3]Vision Team information on www.disciples.org.

[4]*Program of the Centennial*, 11.

[5]Dietrich Bonhoeffer, *Letters and Papers from Prison*, rev. ed. (New York: MacMillian Co., 1967), 172.

[6]Ibid., 211.

Chapter 2: Covenant

[1]C. Leonard Allen, "Congregational Life and Discipline: An Historical Perspective," *Mid-Stream* 26, no. 3 (July 1987): 379.

[2]Alexander Campbell, quoted in Nathan O. Hatch, *The Democratization of American Christianity* (New Haven: Yale University Press, 1989), 76.

[3]Thomas Campbell, *Declaration and Address*, and Barton W. Stone and Others, *Last Will and Testament of the Springfield Presbytery*, with brief introduction by F.D. Kerchner (St. Louis: Bethany Press, 1955), 42. Barton Stone makes a similar point in ibid., 18.

[4]*Program of the International Centennial Celebration and Conventions of the Disciples of Christ* (Cincinnati: American Christian Missionary Society, 1909), 11.

[5]Ralph G. Wilburn, "Disciple Thought in Protestant Perspective: An Interpretation," in *The Reconstruction of Theology*, ed. R.G. Wilburn, vol. 2 of *The Renewal of the Church: The Panel Reports*, ed. W.B. Blakemore (St. Louis: Bethany Press, 1963), 307.

[6]Allen, "Congregational Life and Discipline," 385.

[7]Paul Blowers, "Liberty," in *The Encyclopedia of the Stone-Campbell Movement*, ed. Douglas A. Foster, Paul M. Blowers, Anthony L. Dunnavant, and D. Newell Williams (Grand Rapids, Mich.: Eerdmans, 2004), 477.

[8]This is the language of the Salem Church Covenant of 1629.

[9]Ronald E. Osborn, "Theological Issues in the Restructure of the Christian Church (Disciples of Christ)," *Mid-Stream*, Vol. 19, no. 3 (July 1980): 296.

[10]Text of *The Design* available through www.disciples.org.

[11]Robert Bellah, Richard Madsen, William M. Sullivan, Ann Swidler, Steven M. Tipton, *Habits of the Heart: Individualism and Commitment in American Life* (Berkeley: Univ. of California Press, 1985).

[12]Dean R. Hoge, Benton Johnson, and Donald A. Luidens, *Vanishing Boundaries* (Louisville: Westminster John Knox Press, 1994), 141.

¹³Gary Dorrien, *Soul in Society* (Minneapolis: Fortress Press, 1995), 365.

¹⁴Clark Williamson, "Theological Reflection and Disciples Renewal" in *Disciples of Christ in the 21ˢᵗ Century,* ed. Michael Kinnamon (St. Louis: CBP Press, 1988), 86.

¹⁵Colbert S. Cartwright and O.I. Harrison, *Chalice Worship* (St. Louis: Chalice Press, 1997), 199.

¹⁶Jim Duke, unpublished paper written for the Commission on Theology of the Council on Christian Unity.

¹⁷William Baird, *What Is Our Authority?* (St. Louis: Christian Board of Publication, 1983), 39.

¹⁸Williamson, "Theological Reflection," 101.

Chapter 3: Scripture

¹Alexander Campbell, *The Christian System* (1835; reprint, Salem, N.H.: Ayer Company Publishers, 1988), 15.

²M. Eugene Boring, *Disciples and the Bible: A History of Biblical Disciples Interpretation in North America* (St. Louis: Chalice Press, 1997), 417.

³Ibid., 419–26.

⁴Ibid., 426.

⁵Campbell, *The Christian System,* 15.

⁶See Boring, *Disciples and the Bible,* 85–86. See also Campbell, *The Christian System,* 16–17.

⁷Boring, *Disciples and the Bible,* 105.

⁸Ibid., 19.

⁹Ibid., 409.

¹⁰Ibid., 423–26.

¹¹Albert Outler, ed., *John Wesley* (New York: Oxford Univ. Press, 1964).

¹²In a November 15, 2006, story entitled "Bishops stress sexual issues and warn on Communion," regarding the decision by the Conference of American Bishops to reaffirm the church's stand on birth control, *Boston Globe* writer Michael Paulson stated that the Bishops "acknowledged that most married Catholics—96 percent, according to their own estimate—use birth control."

¹³Ibid., 427–28.

¹⁴Joan Chittister, Mushid Saadi Shakur Chishti, and Arthur Waskow, *The Tent of Abraham* (Boston: Beacon Press, 2006), 6.

¹⁵See Mark G. Toulouse, *Joined in Discipleship* (St. Louis: Chalice Press, 1992).

Chapter 4: The Lord's Supper

¹For a discussion of this issue, see Richard L. Harrison's "Early Disciples Sacramental Theology: Catholic, Reformed, and Free," in *Classic Themes of Disciples Theology: Rethinking the Traditional Affirmations of the Christian Church (Disciples of Christ),* ed. Kenneth Lawrence (Fort Worth, Tex: Texas Christian University Press, 1986).

²Available through www.disciples.org/21stCenturyVisionTeam/ tabid/335 /Default.aspx.

³Alexander Campbell, *The Christian System* (1835; reprint, Salem, New Hampshire: Ayer Company Publishers, 1988), 309.

⁴Ibid.

⁵Barton Stone, *The Christian Messenger,* September 1828, 261–62.

⁶Campbell, *The Christian System,* 310.

⁷Ibid., 306.

⁸Ibid., 305.

[9]Ibid.

[10]Ibid.

[11]Ibid., 316, 312.

[12]Mark G. Toulouse, *Joined in Discipleship* (St. Louis: Chalice Press, 1992),124.

[13]Campbell, *The Christian System*, 311.

[14]Ibid., 301.

[15]Toulouse, *Joined in Discipleship*, 122.

[16]James O. Duke and Richard L Harrison Jr., *The Lord's Supper* (St. Louis: Christian Board of Publication, 1993), 43.

[17]Nils Dahl, *Jesus in the Memory of the Early Church* (Minneapolis: Augsburg, 1976).

[18]Ibid., 20.

[19]Ibid., 21.

[20]Barton W. Stone, *The Christian Messenger*, 1, no. 1. (November 1826): 5–17.

[21]Toulouse, *Joined in Discipleship*, 125, points out that the Disciples Council on Christian Unity's Commission on Theology, in its "Word to the Church on the Lord's Supper," presented to the 1991 Tulsa General Assembly, suggested that the prayers of elders at the table should include a petition for the presence of the Holy Spirit.

[22]Dallas Willard, *Renovation of the Heart* (Colorado Springs: NAVPress, 2002).

[23]For a discussion of this issue coming before the General Assembly, see Michael Kinnamon, "Authority in the Church: Envisioning the Answers," *Lexington Quarterly*, Volume 40, Number 1 (Spring 2005): 16. Also, articles taking divergent views on unbaptized children and Communion are included in the Summer, Fall, and Winter 2005 issues of the *Lexington Quarterly* by Sharon Warner, Jerry Sumney, and Sharyn Dowd respectively.

Chapter 5: Baptism

[1]The COCU Consensus (Consultation on Church Union, 1985), 37.

[2]Stephen J. England, "Toward a Theology of Baptism" in *The Revival of the Churches*, vol. 3 of *The Renewal of the Church: The Panel Reports*, ed. W.B. Blakemore (St. Louis: Bethany Press, 1963), 190.

[3]Clark M. Williamson, *Baptism: Embodiment of the Gospel* (St. Louis: Christian Board of Publication, 1987), 38 and 39.

[4]See Douglas A. Foster, Paul M. Blowers, Anthony L. Dunnavant, and D. Newell Williams, eds., *The Encyclopedia of the Stone-Campbell Movement*, ed. (Grand Rapids, Mich.: Eerdmans, 2004), 60; and Mark G. Toulouse, *Joined in Discipleship* (St. Louis: Chalice Press, 1992), 112.

[5]Alexander Campbell, *The Christian System* (St. Louis: Christian Publishing Co., 1835), 199–200.

[6]Alexander Campbell, as cited in Williamson, *Baptism*, 38, and "A Word to the Church on Baptism: Report of the Commission on Theology, 1987" in Williamson, *Baptism*, 49–50.

[7]*Encyclopedia*, p. 58.

[8]See www.disciplesscouter.org/files/TheDesign.pdf.

[9]Lesslie Newbigin, *The Other Side of 1984* (Geneva: WCC, 1984), 35.

[10]Leander E. Keck, *Romans* (Nashville: Abingdon Press, 2005), 161.

[11]United Church of Christ, *Book of Worship* (New York : United Church of Christ, Office for Church Life and Leadership, 1986).

[12]Keith Watkins, ed., *Baptism and Belonging* (St. Louis: Chalice Press, 1991), 67–88.

Chapter 6: Unity

[1]Peter Ainslie, *The Message of the Disciples of Christ for the Union of the Church* (New York: Fleming H. Revell Co., 1913), 19.

[2]Thomas J. Liggett, "Why Disciples Chose Unity," *Mid-Stream*, 19, no. 2 (April 1980): 228.

[3]Thomas Campbell, *Declaration and Address* (1809; reprint, St. Louis: Bethany Press, 1955), 44.

[4]Program of the International Centennial Celebration and Conventions of the Disciples of Christ (Cincinnati: American Christian Missionary Society, 1909), 10.

[5]Peter Ainslie, quoted in Howard E. Short, *Doctrine and Thought of the Disciples of Christ* (St. Louis: Christian Board of Publication, 1951), 90.

[6]The phrase is from the Identity Statement written by the Disciples Vision Team, which is printed in full in the Appendix.

[7]Ainslie, *The Message*, 22.

[8]Barton Stone, quoted in Lester G. McAllister and William E. Tucker, *Journey in Faith: A History of the Christian Church (Disciples of Christ)* (St. Louis: Bethany Press, 1975), 88.

[9]Thomas Campbell, *Declaration and Address*, 40, 47.

[10]Peter Ainslie, *If Not a United Church—What?* (New York: Fleming H. Revell Co., 1920), 11.

[11]Hampton Adams, *Why I Am a Disciple of Christ* (Boston: Beacon Press, 1957), 109.

[12]Ronald E. Osborn, *Experiment in Liberty* (St. Louis: Bethany Press, 1978), 102.

[13]"Message of the First Assembly of the WCC" (1948), in Michael Kinnamon and Brian E. Cope, eds., *The Ecumenical Movement: An Anthology of Key Text and Voices* (Geneva: WCC, 1997), 21.

[14]Mark G. Toulouse, *Joined in Discipleship* (St. Louis: Chalice Press, 1992), 84.

[15]Ralph G. Wilburn, "The Unity We Seek," in the *Revival of the Churches*, vol. 3 of *The Renewal of the Church: The Panel Reports*, ed. W.B. Blakemore (St. Louis: Bethany Press, 1963), 336.

[16]For a fuller treatment of this theme, see Michael Kinnamon, *The Vision of the Ecumenical Movement and How it Has Been Impoverished by Its Friends* (St. Louis: Chalice Press, 2003), chapter 1.

[17]Robert N. Bellah, et al., *Habits of the Heart* (New York: Harper and Rose, 1985), 244.

[18]Kinnamon and Cope, *Ecumenical Movement*, 469.

[19]William Robinson, *What Churches of Christ Stand For* (Birmingham: Berean Press, 1959), 70.

[20]Alexander Campbell, "Address on War," in Lester G. McAllister, ed., *An Alexander Campbell Reader* (St. Louis: CBP Press, 1988), 103.

[21]See W. B. Garrison and A. T. DeGroot, *The Disciples of Christ: A History* (St. Louis: Christian Board of Publication, 1948), 335.

[22]Craig M. Watts, "A Disciples of Christ Peace Heritage" (unpublished manuscript, Lexington, Ky.: Kentucky Disciples Peace Fellowship, 1998), 1.

[23]Quoted in ibid., 2–3.

[24]Quoted in Craig M. Watts, "Peter Ainslie, Church Unity and the Repudiation of War," *Encounter*, Vol. 68, No. 3 (Summer 2007): 2.

[25]Charles Clayton Morrison, *The Unfinished Reformation* (New York: Harper and Brothers Publishers, 1953), chapter 1.

[26]Quoted in Watts, "Peace Heritage," 9.

[27]William Robinson, *Christianity Is Pacifism* (London: George Allen and

Unwin Ltd., 1933), 97. For further summary of Disciples peace involvements, including the outstanding leadership of Kirby Page, see James A. Crain, *The Development of Social Ideas Among the Disciples of Christ* (St. Louis: Bethany Press, 1969), chapter 5.

[28]Ernst Lange, *And Yet It Moves*, trans. Edwin Robertson (Grand Rapids, Mich.: Eerdmans Publishing, 1979), 147.

[29]This phrase, from the Oxford conference in Church and Society, appeared in the letter inviting churches to become founding members of the WCC. It is quoted in W. W. Visser't Hofft, *Memoirs* (London: SCM Press, 1973), 73.

[30]David Gill, ed., *Gathered for Life: Official Report of the South Assembly of the World Council of Churches* (Geneva: WCC, 1983), 49.

[31]See Harold L. Lunger, the *Political Ethics of Alexander Campbell* (St. Louis: Bethany Press, 1954), 242–63.

[32]Panel on Christian Ethics in a Nuclear Age, *Seeking God's Peace in a Nuclear Age: A Call to Disciples of Christ* (St. Louis: CBP Press, 1985), 54.

[33]Ainslie, *If Not a United Church—What?*, 33.

[34]Peter Ainslie, quoted in Watts, "Peace Heritage," 7.

[35]Jean Vanier, *Community and Growth* (New York: Panelist Press, 1989), 31.

Chapter 7: Mission

[1]Alexander Campbell, *The Christian System* (St. Louis: Christian Publishing Co., 1835), 9.

[2]See Mark G. Toulouse, *Joined in Discipleship* (St. Louis: Chalice Press, 1992), 182–83.

[3]Stanley Hauerwas and Will Willimon, *Resident Aliens* (Nashville: Abingdon Press, 1989).

[4]*Merriam-Webster Online Dictionary*, http://www.merriam-webster.com/dictionary/diverse.

Chapter 8: Congregation

[1]Alexander Campbell, *The Christian System* (1835; reprint, Salem, N.H.: Ayer Company Publishers, 1988), 73–76.

Chapter 9: Leadership

[1]*The Lexington Quarterly*, 41, nos. 3 and 4 (Fall/Winter 2006): 282–83.

[2]Ronald E. Osborn, *In Christ's Place* (St. Louis: The Bethany Press, 1967), 22.

[3]Ibid., 21.

[4]John Gardner, "The Heart of the Matter: Leader-Constituent Interaction," paper no. 3 (Washington, D.C., Independent Sector Leadership Studies Program, June 1986), 5.

[5]Charles Marsh, *WayWard Christian Soldiers* (New York: Oxford University Press, 2007), 98.

[6]Gardner, "The Heart of the Matter," 25.

[7]Ibid.

[8]John Gardner, "The Tasks of Leadership," paper no. 2 (Washington, D.C., Independent Sector Leadership Studies Program, March 1986), 22.

[9]Parker J. Palmer, "Leading from Within: Reflection on Spirituality and Leadership" (Washington, D.C.: The Servant Leadership School, 1990), 3.

[10]Ibid.

[11]Ibid., 4.

[12]Elaine M. Prevalett, "Reflections on Simplicity" (Wallingford, Pa.: Pendle Hill Publications, pamphlet 244, 1982), 5–6.

[13]Ibid., 6.

[14]Robert K. Greenleaf, *Seeker And Servant: Reflections on Religious Leadership,* ed. Anne T. Franker and Larry C. Spears (San Francisco: Jossey-Bass, 1996), 14.

[15]Ibid., 54.

[16]Ibid., 14.

[17]Ibid.